The Power of Intimate Love

Experiencing Sexual Fulfillment In Marriage

by
Karin Brown

Harrison House
Tulsa, Oklahoma

Direct quotations from the Bible appear in bold type.

The Power of Intimate Love:
Experiencing Sexual Fulfillment in Marriage
ISBN 1-57794-007-5

Published by Harrison House, Inc.
P.O. Box 35035
Tulsa, Oklahoma 74153

The Power of Intimate Love

Contents

Introduction

Most people believe they have at least a measure of familiarity with the subject of sexual intimacy—perhaps some even feel comfortable verbalizing their opinions and concerns about it—but far too few married couples really understand the importance of keeping intimacy alive—even vibrant.

It has become essential to me that I do whatever I can to see that Christian couples are given the opportunity to gain a clearer understanding of all the aspects of keeping the sparks flying in the marriage bed.

Open communication is critical to sexual fulfillment. Let me give you just one example of the many testimonials that I have heard through the years. At a Bible study I taught for women, I met a young mother who felt she had a good, strong marriage. During the frank discussion regarding satisfying sexual relationships, this woman confessed that she had never experienced an orgasm in her twelve years of marriage and wondered what all the fuss was about. It didn't seem to her as if there was myrrh to all the "hype" about sex.

After I spoke with her, she went home and talked with her husband. Their simple discussion resulted in an entirely new level of sexual intimacy, which both found quite appealing and pleasing. She experienced total fulfillment for the first time in their relationship.

She even discovered that there are health benefits to be enjoyed between a husband and wife who have a fulfilling sex life. One of the natural benefits of this woman's newfound sexual fulfillment was a total release from tension and pressure. She later told me, "Karin, I'm a new woman. I did not know why I was so frustrated, uptight and tense. I cannot believe the difference in my life now that I am feeling sexually fulfilled."

Her husband related that he'd known he hadn't been pleasing her but didn't know what to do about it. Sadly, they had never discussed their sexual intimacy in twelve years of marriage. Their new commitment to open communication about their sexuality would transform both their marital and individual health.

Her experience, more than anything else, spurred me on to educate people. I believe it is a shame for a lack of knowledge to deprive Christians of the God-given privilege of sexual fulfillment in marriage. God designed sex to be an enjoyable, healthy and satisfying experience for every man and woman.

In addition to the natural benefits of a healthy sexual relationship between husband and wife, there are spiritual benefits as well. After all, sexual intimacy is a covenant act.

Traditionally, covenants have involved an exchange of blood. In many cultures throughout history, participants in covenants slit their wrists and bound them together to allow their blood to mingle while reciting covenant vows. According to God's Word, life is in the blood (Lev. 17:11), so through this covenant act their lives would flow one to another.

Some scientists believe that a man's semen contains a trace of blood so small that it can only be detected under a microscope.[1] Further, when a virgin comes to the marriage bed, there is a releasing of blood when the hymen is broken. Thus, with the consummation of their marriage vows in the act of sexual intimacy, the couple exchange the life flowing within them and become one.

Furthermore, every time a man and a woman come together physically, the covenant is renewed.

The life flowing from one to the other creates a wonderful communion that brings with it the remembrance of their initial feelings of love for one another. It is similar to the times when we take communion with God; we are reminded that there was an exchange of His life for ours and His strengths for our weaknesses.

During the course of our seminars, my husband and I split up the men and women so we can share woman-to-woman and man-to-man.

Sexual intimacy is such a taboo subject for some Christians that many people have become highly offended and have refused to participate in these discussions. This avoidance of the subject of sexual intimacy concerns us, because God himself is the One who ordained the sexual relationship between husbands and wives, and discussions like these could open their hearts to discovering God's plan for even this most intimate part of their marriages.

It is God's desire for every Christian couple to find sexual fulfillment in marriage. As you read on, you will see how important this is to Him and you will discover the joy He intended for you to experience in sexual intimacy with your husband or your wife.

Many Christians don't understand the spiritual aspects of the sexual relationship. They tend to view sex with a strictly worldly connotation rather than as a gift from God.

Gifts usually bring mutual pleasure: The giver is blessed by the opportunity to give, and the recipient is blessed by the act of love expressed in the form of the gift. God's gift of marital intimacy brings pleasure not only to the recipients but also to the Giver, who loves to bless His own.

Just as God would like us to be open, vulnerable and yielding in our interactions with Him, so we should be with our marriage partners. Each time we commune with God in prayer and worship, we feel closer to Him. And each time we join our mates in the marriage bed, a new level of closeness develops. It's called the abundant married life.

My prayer, reader, is for you to draw closer to God as you draw closer to your mate and begin to enjoy your relationship to the fullest.

CHAPTER 1

Feast or Famine?

He brought me to the banqueting house, and his banner over me was love.

Song of Solomon 2:4

We used to sing a praise chorus in church that began, "He brought me to His banqueting table." We accompanied it with hand motions and felt certain we knew exactly what we were singing about.

How surprised we were to discover that instead of extolling God's love for us, we were singing a verse that literally referred to a man's love for his bride! We were shocked to read further and realize that the next few verses actually described with intimate detail the sexual foreplay King Solomon and his beloved, the Shulamite, enjoyed.

The more we read, the more incredulous we became. Could there be a whole book in the Bible devoted to a couple's love life, complete with explicit details of their lovemaking experiences? Would the Bible actually cover such a topic?

Soon, we realized that the Song of Solomon was indeed a beautiful love story packed with vivid descriptions of every aspect of satisfying sexual intimacy. It is one of the best textbooks for sexual instruction ever printed. Of course, knowledge of the Hebrew language helps, but even a novice can see through the King James English with a little imagination.

This interpretation of the Song of Solomon stands in contrast with the view that it is an allegory of the love relationship between God and Israel, Christ and the church or Christ and the soul. It also controverts the more modern interpretations which see it as a love story between a shepherd lover and his beloved maiden who refuses to be won over by the flatteries and allurements of the king to become part of his harem because she is pledged to another.[1] Yet after a careful examination of the Song of Solomon, I believe it is the story of the intimate love between King Solomon and the Shulamite.

Each of us, whether male or female, was created with an appetite for sex. It was God who thought up "the urge to merge," as I like to call it. Genesis 2:24 records His declaration of this design: **Therefore shall a man leave his father and his mother, and shall cleave unto his wife: and they shall be one flesh.**

In the Song of Solomon 2:4, the Shulamite joyously proclaims, **He brought me to the banqueting house.** Yet, despite God's design, far too few men and women ever experience sexual intimacy as a satisfying feast. For some, it is unappealing and unsatisfying. Others might compare their sex lives to famine: They are starving, and consequently their marriages are in poor health.

Over the years my husband and I have ministered to thousands of couples and singles in Christian marriage seminars. We have concluded that one of the reasons so many marriages are suffering from the "famine syndrome" is due to the lack of understanding that exists within the Christian community regarding sex.

How do we become good lovers to each other? How should we respond to one another? How does a couple maintain the life-giving relationship of sexual intimacy throughout the length of a marriage? Is abundant life to be found in the marriage relationship?

Let's explore some possibilities and discover what may be dousing the flame in so many Christian marriages.

HOW WOULD YOU RATE YOUR SEX LIFE?

Is your sex life a feast or a famine? Is it immensely satisfying, or is malnutrition far too familiar? Or is your sex life unappetizing, uninteresting or uncomfortable?

You may consider it in poor taste to compare sexual intimacy with feasting, but perhaps reading the Song of Solomon will serve to enlighten your thinking.

In chapter 4, Solomon appreciatively describes his delight in his bride's body. With one metaphor after another, he describes her beautiful eyes, hair, teeth and so forth. He compares her temples to pomegranates, her lips to dripping honeycombs and her tongue to a source of honey and milk. (vv. 3,11.) He speaks of her as a garden with pomegranates and pleasant fruits and spices. (vv. 12,13.) In verse 16, she bids him to come into his garden and eat his pleasant fruits.

And Solomon was not the only one making such comparisons. In chapter 2, verse 3, the Shulamite compares her husband to an apple tree and says that his fruit is sweet to her taste.

But it doesn't stop here. The comparison between feasting and enjoying sexual delights continues throughout the Song of Solomon and still serves as a suitable metaphor today. Just as good food nourishes you, a good sex life will nourish your marriage and your personal life. A delectable meal is seasoned perfectly, served sizzling hot and appeals to the eye as well as the palate. So should your sexually intimate times be.

How Would Your Mate Rate Your Sex Life?

Maybe you would describe your sex life as a famine, but your mate thinks it is more like a feast. In that case, you might be guilty of answering that old proverbial question, "Was it good for you too?" either unfavorably or dishonestly.

How could two people view the same experience so differently? One reason is the basic differences between male and female thinking and sexual needs.

If the woman describes her sex life as a famine, she may not be talking about the number of times she has sex in a week but of the quality of the experiences. Perhaps she has never, or rarely, experienced orgasms but her husband still thoroughly enjoys sex with her each time.

If her husband is ignorant of her need for foreplay to arouse her sexually or simply is ignorant of how to stimulate her but is still experiencing fulfillment every time, then to him their love life may be more like a feast.

Suppose the woman is interested in intercourse, but because her husband moves too fast, she rarely achieves an orgasm. Frustration and resentment may begin to set in. She genuinely desires a more fulfilling sexual experience but is afraid to talk to her mate about it. For her, their love life is still famine or, at best, an unsatisfying meal.

Can you imagine how difficult it would be for a starving person to watch another receiving all of the nourishment he or she needs at a meal? Suppose that person not only had to watch but actually had to serve those meals to the other on a regular basis. Pretty soon the starving person would probably be tempted to become bitter, angry, jealous and maybe even hateful of the other. He or she may have felt love for the other originally, but his or her own lack has caused resentment.

It seems unthinkable for the above scenario to happen in this country in which equality is so very important, but it does every day. The ones who are starving are love hungry—starving for attention, affection and sexual satisfaction. Eventually, they're tempted to become frustrated, resentful and angry with their mates who can enjoy sexual satisfaction without the handicaps.

As my husband and I have traveled and taught on marriage, I have met many women who are the starving ones. Yet their mates may still view their sex lives as satisfying feasts. Perhaps these husbands receive their regular helpings of satisfying sexual intimacy but are insensitive to, or simply unaware of, their wives' specific needs. So out of their own frustration, their wives may regularly endure but not enjoy. If their husbands are aware of their wives' lack, they suffer with them, disappointed that they are unable to satisfy their wives' needs.

We have also met many men who are starving, not only for love and attention, but for the ability to perform sexually. Many men are unable to maintain erections, yet they are either too proud or too ashamed to seek help. They may be having problems with impotency due to prescription medications, smoking, alcohol, substance abuses or psychological problems. Whatever the reason, their wives suffer with them.

WOMEN'S NEEDS

You should know that God intended for husbands and wives to enjoy one another in every way and to give themselves wholeheartedly to each other—spirit, soul and body—without any hindrances. But you should also know that God created men and woman differently, so they approach sexual intimacy in different ways.

The Shulamite illustrates how important it is for a woman to feel secure, loved, cherished and protected in order to freely give of herself sexually to her husband. In the Song of Solomon 2:3, she illustrates her sense of security when, after comparing her beloved to an apple tree, she says that she **sat down under his shadow with great delight.** The word *shadow* denotes shade, protection and covering.[2]

A sense of security is essential for a woman, because when she begins to climax, she has the sense of losing control completely. Subconsciously, unless she feels secure and loved, she could resist that climax and sexually shut herself down.

Some women experience this because of past traumatic sexual experiences, such as having been victims of molestation or rape. Their insecurities in lovemaking may have nothing to do with their husbands but, instead, may be the result of a general lack of trust in men, for whatever reason. Together, a husband and wife should patiently and lovingly deal with these issues through discussion or, if need be, through godly counsel.

Some women are insecure about their physical appearances. Solomon's bride, the Shulamite, was a dark-skinned country girl during a time when a measure of value was placed on the fairness of a young girl's skin. The

Shulamite worked in her brother's fields before her prince charming swept her away to his palace. She said, **Look not upon me, because I am black, because the sun hath looked upon me: my mother's children were angry with me; they made me the keeper of the vineyards; but mine own vineyard have I not kept** (Song 1:6).

Despite what she or others might have called her "flaws," Solomon lavishly doted on her with great charm and gentle love. He provided for his bride's every need and romanced her often. His affection gave her the self-assurance she needed to feel secure in his arms and to let herself be truly satisfied by his embrace.

According to the NIV *Study Bible,* the ancient Semitic languages sometimes interchanged the letters "l" and "n," making *Shulamite* either a variant of "Shunammite," i.e., a girl from Shunem, or a feminine form of the word *Solomon,* meaning "Solomon's girl."[3] *Halley's Bible Handbook* says that the Shulamite was most probably Solomon's favorite wife and that this particular song was written to celebrate his marriage to her.[4]

When the Shulamite said, **He brought me to the banqueting house, and his banner over me was love** (Song 2:4), she may have been referring to the bridal feast, which normally took place in the bridal chambers, or bedroom. Or she may have been referring to a place where feasts were held, because *banqueting house* in the Hebrew literally translates "house of wine."[5] Because of Solomon's position as king, we can assume that at some point there was a lavish wedding celebration, complete with the finest food available. It would undoubtedly make our most elaborate wedding receptions look meager in every way.

The wedding celebration was probably overwhelming to the Shulamite, but I believe she was describing something much more intimate and sensual than that. I believe the feast she referred to in this verse was that of sexual pleasure, not food.

The fact that the young bride spoke of Solomon's banner over her tells us even more. A *banner* was a pole with a cloth attached, much like a flag. It was used in many ways in Scripture—sometimes as a mark of identity. The banner over Solomon's banqueting house identified it as his own. And his banner over her identified her as the object of his love, which provided security, care and protection.[6]

In other words, the Shulamite was saying that her beloved had already given her protection, that she felt secure in his love and that she was his entirely. As she entered into the banqueting hall, she was very aware that all attention was focused on her. She would be identified from this time on as his.

These are all prerequisites to a woman's yielding herself freely to a man.

So, through her words, she indicated her eagerness to be his totally on this, her wedding night. Solomon and the Shulamite's wedding night was a marathon of lovemaking that lasted all night long, based on the love and security that he offered. This love was then consummated in a powerfully sensual melding together of the two—body, soul and spirit. It permeated every part of their beings and had all the elements needed to qualify it as a great love feast: romance, desire, tenderness, passionate arousal and fulfillment.

MEN'S NEEDS

While love and security are important for a woman to feel before she can find true sexual fulfillment, a man gains a greater connection with his own emotions after he joins his wife intimately. After making himself more vulnerable and open to her physically, he then rediscovers how much he loves her and how connected he feels with her emotionally.

In addition, his male ego is greatly influenced by how well he performs sexually. When he and his wife are sexually satisfied, he is "on top of the world." If he is impotent, though, his sense of oneness with his wife and deep love for her seem to be absent; his own emotions seem to be far away.

If weeks, months or even years go by with no sexual satisfaction between him and his wife, he may grow cold and insensitive toward her. She, in turn, because of her own need for sexual completion, will feel a deep void. She may be frustrated, uptight, nervous and unsatisfied.

Because both have great needs for fulfillment that should be satisfied through sexual connection with one another, they both may be tempted to turn elsewhere.

Much will depend on their individual commitments to God, each other and their marriage. If their commitments are weak, they may try to fill the void with work, hobbies, sports, extramarital affairs or other activities that can never replace God's design of sexual intimacy between husband and wife.

Considering these options, can you see how devastating sexual dysfunction can be? God intended fulfillment, satisfaction, unity, strength and ecstasy to thrive in the marriage bed. But if, instead, there is division, defeat, humiliation, lack and frustration, the ramifications can be terribly destructive.

When we really understand men's and women's need for becoming "one flesh," is it any wonder that God commanded this when He instituted marriage? (Gen. 2:24.) God expected husbands and wives to enjoy sexual relations for as long as they were together.

It is Satan who steals, kills and destroys. It is Satan who brings about famine. It is Satan who authors mediocre, dull, boring sexual experiences.

If God is in it, it is good. If God is in it, it will prosper. If God is in it, it will be in abundance and bring fulfillment.

DEALING WITH SEXUAL INACTIVITY

Perhaps there is no sexual activity in your marriage, for whatever reason, and you are thinking, *Well, our marriage*

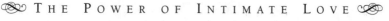

is just fine without it. No, it isn't, because God clearly shows us in His Word that we are to be one flesh. You may still have love going for you, but you don't have God's best without fulfillment in this area. That isn't abundant living.

Conversely, if your sex life is completely inactive because you are single, you may be wondering what to do with your sexual frustrations, especially if you were once sexually active. You may be wondering how you can experience the abundant life without sex. Well, Jesus did it, and so did Paul. And while it is true that they *chose* their single status, they also chose to remain celibate.

While there are many Scriptures concerning putting the flesh under, let me give you one very practical piece of advice: Try exercising as an alternative to sex and for relief from frustration and tension. Exercise has been effective for persons who have come to me for counseling, even those who were battling homosexual urges. Used in addition to prayer and the Word of God, exercise can help you experience the strength needed to remain pure until marriage.

Fill your life with God, set your desires in order with His and find good, godly friends with whom to fellowship and fill your need for companionship.

ENJOY GOD'S BEST IN THE MARRIAGE BED

While I am not attempting to overemphasize the need for an active and satisfying sex life in marriage—there are many other important aspects of marriage also discussed in God's Word— we all need to recognize the important role sexual intimacy does play.

If God didn't think a flourishing sexual relationship between husband and wife was important, why would He have given Adam the command in Genesis 2:24 to **cleave unto his wife** immediately after Eve was created for him? *Cleave* means "to stick as things that are glued together."[7] If you are really cleaving to your husband or your wife, then you will never stop chasing him or her. Then God completes this command with the words, **and they shall be one flesh.** That command has never been and will never be rescinded.

Whether your present sex life is wonderful, mediocre, unbearable or simply boring, this book was written with you in mind.

It was designed to whet your appetite, to tantalize your taste buds, to transform your leftovers into delicious feasts and to instruct those of you who just need to start cooking.

Whether you are in a feast or famine right now, read on. When you finish this cookbook and follow the godly instructions to add the proper ingredients of love, faith and patience, you will be sure to have a more delectable meal than you have ever had before.

CHAPTER 2

Finer Than Wine

Let him kiss me with the kisses of his mouth: for thy love is better than wine.

Song of Solomon 1:2

In Bible times a feast always included fine wines. This is still customary today in many cultures around the world. Wine, at its best, is supposed to be clear in color, fragrant, full-bodied, smooth—whether sweet or dry—and subtly intoxicating. Wine connoisseurs say wine should be sipped slowly, served with the proper meat according to color, aged to perfection and placed in wine goblets at room temperature.

Wine has long been associated with love, romance, wooing and pursuing. The familiar term "wining and dining" was, at one time, associated with the preliminaries leading to sexual foreplay. It set the stage for consummated love at its best, according to worldly standards.

SOLOMON'S LOVE WAS FINER THAN WINE

When the Shulamite spoke of King Solomon's kisses and his love as being better than wine, she meant they were more intoxicating, more flavorful and more enjoyable than any wine served in his palace. Considering the expensive and rare wines that would have been served in the palace of a king, you can see that this was quite a compliment.

In chapter 1, verse 4, the Shulamite continues to speak of the pleasures of their lovemaking, saying:

> **Draw me, we will run after thee: the king hath brought me into his chambers: we will be glad and rejoice in thee, we will remember thy love more than wine....**

Did you notice how she referred to their approaching time in the king's chambers, or the bedroom? It would not only be a glad, rejoicing time but would later be remembered more than one could recall fine wine. It would last longer and bring greater enjoyment. In fact, she would again receive pleasure just thinking about it.

Long after she remembered the merriment of any feast, the taste of the finest wines and the excitement of great celebrations and festivities, she would reminisce Solomon's love in her heart, her thoughts and even her body. So intoxicating were his love and sexual intimacy with her that they would have long-lasting effects. Even the memory of them would be better than the finest wine.

The afterglow of their lovemaking would reach far beyond the average span of thirty minutes. She would sense it as she fell asleep, would dream of her beloved all night and would arise with a secret smile on her face that began deep down in her heart. Her inner being would glow at the very thought of her beloved king, and her body would become aroused remembering the wonderful things that had happened the night before in their bed. She would feel more connected to her husband, more in love with him, more secure in his love for her, more committed to him, more desirous of him and more determined to demonstrate her deep love for him.

And somewhere, deep inside her, she knew God had created their love to bring this deep satisfaction. Somewhere, if she was spiritually inclined, she knew there was more to this great mystery of sexual connection than she yet understood. Somehow, she felt God's love and purpose for her womanhood had been fulfilled as she and Solomon expressed their love together freely.

With the Shulamite's emotional stability at its best and her spiritual awareness increasing, her body would inevitably feel better too. She was no longer tense or even anxious. Just as wine was said to be good for the stomach, a pleasurable sexual encounter was soothing to her physical being. She felt spiritually, mentally and physically whole.

A REMINDER OF THE BLOOD COVENANT

While I may have interjected some possibilities that aren't technically described in the Song of Solomon, they really aren't so far-fetched. You can read most of them between the lines.

And even though not much is mentioned in the Song of Solomon about the act of marriage being covenantal in nature, it most certainly is; sexual intimacy carries with it tremendous spiritual significance.

Webster's New World College Dictionary defines *covenant* as "1) a binding and solemn agreement to do or keep from doing a specified thing; compact; 2) an agreement among members of a church to defend and maintain its doctrines, polity, and faith; 3) a formal, sealed contract; 4) the promise made by God to man, as recorded in the Bible."[1]

In his book *The Blood Covenant*, H. Clay Trumball records his extensive research of covenants, particularly blood covenants, between two primitive tribes. According to his research, whenever such covenants were ratified, they were accompanied by a cutting, or letting, of blood. When the two parties came together to ratify the covenant they had agreed upon, they would usually recut and allow their blood to flow together.

As their blood intermingled, they would recite their vows to one another. Sometimes they would even let their blood flow into a goblet of wine and then drink from it together because they believed that the life was in the blood. So binding were these vows that if either party broke or even attempted to break the conditions of the vows, persons in their families or tribes may have even hunted them down and killed them. A covenant such as this was made to last forever and was considered the strongest contract known to man and God.

After discovering this practice among primitive tribes, Trumball took his research one step further. He suggested that the blood covenant formed the basis for God's covenant with Abraham, the sacrificial system, the Passover and even the covenant God made with man through the precious shed blood of His Son, Jesus. To show how Old Testament men and women of faith perceived the blood, Trumball pointed to Leviticus 17:11, which says, **the life of the flesh is in the blood.** A major difference, however, was that God strictly forbade the drinking of blood and only allowed the shedding of the blood of animals.[2] (See Lev. 17:10.)

Assuming Trumball was correct in making these connections, each time we partake of the fruit of the vine in our communion services, that juice, which represents Jesus' blood, should not only be taken in remembrance of Him but also in remembrance of the covenant that was cut with Him.

THE MARRIAGE COVENANT

Marriage is so important to God that He set it up as a covenant relationship comparable to this covenant established between Christ and His church.

Just as God and His children share covenant rights, so do husbands and wives. When a man leaves his parents to join his wife, he becomes the covenant head of his household. He and his wife become one flesh as they offer their bodies to one another in the act of sexual intercourse. The husband and wife provide protection, support, security and strength for one another.

Cutting a blood covenant means giving oneself to another. Again, the basis of the blood covenant is that there is life in the blood. The passing of blood from one to another brings about the blending of two spirits, souls and bodies as one.

It is part of God's divine plan for a blood covenant to be established between husband and wife. According to God's wondrous design, a fold of mucous membrane, the hymen, partially closes the external orifice of the vagina. When the bodies of the bride and groom join in the act of intercourse for the first time, the hymen breaks, causing blood to flow. This blood is a sign of the covenant they have cut together.

In many Eastern cultures, even today, the token of the woman's virginity is given to the bride's parents in the form of a cloth with blood on it. It is to serve as proof of her maidenly virginity and evidence that a covenant has been made.[3]

HEALTH BENEFITS OF A GOOD SEX LIFE

When we partake of the covenant meal, we can believe God for the healing of our flesh as we take the bread, and for the forgiveness of our sins as we take the juice. When the Israelites partook of the covenant meal and placed the blood of the lamb on their doorposts, the angel of death passed over them and they were able to walk out of Egypt completely delivered from the bondage of slavery.

Sexual intercourse between husband and wife is designed to do the same, except on a different level. The implications are all there: deliverance from the enemy's tactics (because sexual intimacy brings such union) and protection from death (scientists have identified many health benefits engendered by a good sex life).

Better Relaxation

One benefit that sexual intercourse brings is relaxation from the day's tense activities on the job and at home. Thus, it aids in effecting a good night's sleep. According to Dr. Alexander Lowen, "Sex is a great relaxer. The better and more vigorous, the easier it becomes to fall asleep."[4]

Several years ago my husband and I studied materials in a Jewish synagogue library in preparation for a marriage seminar. We wanted to see what the ancient writings had to say about sex and marriage. One of the most interesting and revealing writings concerned the Sabbath instructions. The men were to read the Song of Solomon on the Sabbath eve and partake of sexual intercourse on the Sabbath. The Sabbath was a holy day set apart for rest and relaxation; intercourse was considered a holy act, to be partaken of on a holy day.[5]

Healthier Heart

Sex is also good for the heart. According to a study reported in a *Reader's Digest* article, 65 of 100 women who had been treated for heart attacks reported feeling sexual dissatisfaction before hospitalization. Another study, according to the same article, found that two-thirds of the 131 men questioned had experienced significant sexual problems before their heart attacks.[6]

According to psychiatrist Alexander Lowen, director of the International Institute for Bioenergetic Analysis in New York City and author of *Love, Sex, and Your Heart,* "A lack of sexual satisfaction should be considered for further study as a possible risk factor for heart disease."[7]

Improved Immune System

Fulfilling, intimate sexual encounters even improve the immune system. Dr. Dudley Chapman, clinical professor of obstetrics and gynecology at Ohio University College of Osteopathic Medicine, found that those "who were content with the intimacy in their lives had better levels of T-cells—the white blood cells that play a major role in the workings of the immune system—and lived longer."[8]

Stress hampers the immune system, making the body more susceptible to diseases, such as cancer, and sicknesses as simple as the common cold. A satisfying sexual experience, however, counters stress and causes total body relaxation. Even though the effects last only a few hours, regular fulfilling sexual intimacy will make a husband and a wife feel progressively healthier and less stressed.

Fewer Aches and Pains

"Orgasm is a natural analgesic," says Beverly Whipple, associate professor at Rutgers University's College of Nursing. In Whipple's study of women who suffered from painful conditions such as chronic arthritis and even whiplash, orgasmic women had significantly raised thresholds of pain. This makes sense, because orgasm causes the central nervous system to release certain chemicals into the body that block pain.[9]

Dr. Dudley Chapman, whom I mentioned earlier in the chapter, reported that one of his female patients who suffered with severe arthritis found that her pain began to diminish after she resumed sexual relations with her husband.[10]

Decreased Symptoms of Premenstrual Syndrome

Many women suffer from premenstrual syndrome. Much of the physiological discomfort of premenstrual syndrome comes five to seven days preceding a woman's period. During this time, the flow of blood to the pelvic area increases, often causing bloating and menstrual cramping.

However, according to Dr. Alfred Franger, associate professor of obstetrics, gynecology and psychiatry at the Medical College of Wisconsin, "Muscle contractions during orgasm force blood to flow rapidly away from the pelvic region and back into general circulation, loosening tightness.[11] What a practical, healing God is He who created such a pleasurable way to alleviate this natural discomfort.

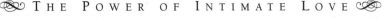

Calorie Reduction

Intercourse is an effective way to burn calories. Dr. Franger says, "Vigorous sex is like a mini-workout." A 120-pound woman can burn up to eight calories a minute, while a 180-pound man can burn up to twelve calories every minute.[12] So sex can even help us with weight control. Every calorie counts!

Improved Mental Health

In 1970, researchers at San Francisco's Institute for Advanced Study of Human Sexuality began a study in which they have now analyzed 37,500 adults. According to their research, people who experience fulfilling sex lives are less anxious, less violent, less hostile and not as likely to blame others for misfortune.[13]

Clinical psychologist Douglas Heath, author of *Fulfilling Lives,* studied sixty-five men and forty women and found that sexual satisfaction also helps to make one more self-reliant. Heath believes this is because "over time, spouses learn how to express their needs, which helps them become less inhibited, more spontaneous, and better able to meet demands."[14]

Roger Falge, a marriage therapist in San Rafael, California, says, "A tender sex life helps bring out in each other the best qualities we have."[15] And when that happens, it is easier to receive healing in both the soul and the body.

Procreation and Pleasure

Having taught on the many spiritual, mental and physical benefits of sexual satisfaction, I could hardly contain my exasperation when I recently listened to a tape by a minister who was speaking to his congregation about sex. He said, "Why does it matter if a woman has an orgasm? Why such a big deal about it anyway?" I would have stopped listening if I hadn't been asked to critique it for the ministry we were a part of. But I wondered what this man's wife and other women in his congregation felt as they heard those selfish words.

There was no mention of men not experiencing fulfillment, nor any comments on the pleasures of both the husband and wife being fulfilled together as one flesh. He only spoke of the need to bring children into this world, as if that were God's only motive for placing sexual desires within us.

This, of course, isn't the only reason God created sex. He created it to be pleasurable just as much as He created it for procreation, and orgasms are a part of that pleasure. Though this pastor didn't seem to think so, I know of one woman who did.

After twelve years of marriage, she and her husband had given birth to three children, but she had never had an orgasm. Eventually she wondered, *Is this all there is to it?* but never said it to her husband. In fact, they had never discussed their sex life during their twelve years of marriage. The wife was in a Bible study in which I taught on the woman's responsibility in preparing herself for intercourse, and I just barely mentioned the fact that men needed to know how to arouse their wives through clitoral stimulation.

That evening, this woman talked with her husband about what I had said and told him of her own sexual dissatisfaction. He confessed he'd inwardly known she wasn't satisfied but simply didn't know how to arouse her. So that night, for the first time in twelve years, they both enjoyed their lovemaking.

She called me a few days later, absolutely rejoicing. She could not get over the difference having orgasms had made in her life. She said, "I was always so nervous, uptight and frustrated, but I never knew why. Now I'm a new person. All my frustrations and tensions are gone."

SEXUAL INTIMACY—FINER THAN WINE

Just as drinking fine wine in Bible days was considered enriching, relaxing and enjoyable, so God has intended sexual intimacy to be in our lives. He created intercourse to be pleasurable, to reach maximum sensual heights and to bring an intimacy level in marriage that yields security and contentment. But He didn't stop there. He also designed it to bring total relaxation, deliverance from stress-filled days, relief from tension, health and healing to our physical bodies, longevity to our lives and extreme pleasure to our souls.

And in addition to all of that, He planned for our spiritual well-being, which is even far more significant.

What a wondrous God we serve who created the "one flesh" principle for us to enjoy, to bring harmony and one-ness in our marriages and intimacy that has spiritual, emotional and physical benefits that go far beyond what we can even imagine. Yes, the Shulamite was right: Love is much finer than even the finest of wines.

CHAPTER 3

Arousal Assumptions

His left hand is under my head, and his right hand doth embrace me.

Song of Solomon 2:6

Why is it that we usually assume because *we* enjoy or need a particular thing that others will too? People often give others gifts that they themselves want, rather than finding out what others really desire. Far too often, that same principle operates in marriage, but the problem this causes in marriage in particular is that God created men and women with different desires and needs.

We are all created with the need for love, affection and acceptance, but the differences lie in how we best express and receive these needs. If a husband doesn't know how to relate his desires to his wife in a way that she receives best, or vice versa, and if one doesn't understand the other's needs well enough to address them, assumptions will be made and dissatisfaction will abound.

WHAT DO YOU WANT?

In the Song of Solomon 2:6, cited above, the Shulamite is specifying what she wants from her husband. But, first, she lets him know exactly what she is thinking. In chapter 2, verse 5, she says, **Stay me with flagons, comfort me with apples: for I am sick of love.** Flagons are raisin cakes. Both raisins and apples are symbols of erotic passion.

In Solomon's day, a popular belief prevailed that raisins enhanced the possibility of conception because they were considered the "seeds" that increased the "seed" of a couple. Hosea 3:1 also speaks of raisin cakes being used in pagan fertility rituals, implying that children would result.

Juicy, ripe apples, abundantly packed with seeds, were thought of as an aphrodisiac relative to the fruitfulness of the human body.[1]

The Shulamite ends her statement by saying, "I am sick of love," which means she is what today we call "lovesick." She is telling him she is passionate for and desirous of him.[2]

In chapter 2, verse 6, when the Shulamite says, **His left hand is under my head, and his right hand doth embrace me**, she is specifically expressing what she wants Solomon to do to satisfy her passion. When she asks him to embrace her, she is literally requesting that he caress her in a loving, intimate way that will arouse her most at the moment.[3]

A woman must clearly express to her husband what she wants sexually, especially during foreplay. If she does not, then how can she expect him to meet her desires or arouse her in the way she most needs at the time? Women should respond to their husband's foreplay by some sort of verbal communication. If she can't easily talk about what she likes, she can let him know what pleases her by other nonverbal communication, such as breathing harder, moaning or squealing.

Women can also help their husbands know what pleases them by complimenting them afterwards on their lovemaking skills, telling them what they did that was particularly arousing.

It is much better to be positive and complimentary about the things that he does right than to respond negatively. Positive feedback will encourage him. Since men love a challenge, if a man's wife says something like, "Honey, I don't know how it could get any better," then he will do his best to make it better the next time.

Conversely, negative feedback may only bring discouragement and wound a man's ego, preventing him from trying something different. Praise always works best.

If you have a good, open relationship with your husband, there is nothing wrong with diplomatically telling him what it is you prefer and what simply doesn't work for you. While the method you use in communicating your sexual needs is important, it isn't as important as the actual communication itself.

A supportive husband needs and wants to know what pleases his wife. He longs to bring her sexual fulfillment. So a loving wife must openly relate her desires to him.

Every Day Is a New Day

Another reason a woman needs to be specific in expressing what she likes is that her preferences may differ from day to day. One day she might really be aroused by breast stimulation—the caressing and kissing of the breasts. Maybe this will arouse her so much that clitoral stimulation will be unnecessary. But, a few days later, when her breasts are swollen because menstruation is nearing, she may not want her breasts touched a whole lot. This time she may want just a very gentle, tender caress on her breasts but more clitoral stimulation.

Another thing for both husbands and wives to remember is that the length of time required for foreplay can widely differ, depending upon which day it is in the wife's menstrual cycle. When a woman is ovulating, she may quickly become passionate and need very little stimulation before she is ready for intercourse, but later on in the month, it could take her twice as long to become sufficiently aroused for climax to be possible.

There may even be times when she knows she is too tired to reach a climax but wants to fulfill her mate's needs. In this case, a loving wife will simply tell the truth.

She will assure him that she can enjoy giving to him in this way on occasion. The old scriptural adage "It is better to give than to receive" (Acts 20:35) comes into play here, and God will reward a wife for this act of love when it is done ungrudgingly and truly in adoration of her husband. If she will pray, asking God to help her respond to her husband's desires, God will never fail her.

As women, our willingness to respond to our husband's needs will produce a spark in our love lives because it is unselfish and loving. Love never fails.

However, a word of caution is necessary: Having intercourse without an orgasm can be frustrating for a woman if it happens too often. Therefore, this should be the exception, not the rule.

Women Need a Reason

The well-known comedian Billy Crystal is quoted as saying that women need a reason for sex, but men just need a place. While I know most married men need more than a place and they, too, need a reason for desiring sex, there is some truth to that statement.

Women need to be given a reason to participate in sexual intimacy. They are responders, so they must have something to respond to before they can be aroused or interested in making love. This is why foreplay is so important.

Foreplay can begin as early as the morning of the night that a husband wants to make passionate love with his wife. He can begin to arouse her by kissing her sensually while whispering exciting promises of things to come that evening.

If that morning he has done a good job of expressing his intentions to please her, she will begin to prepare herself and probably think of it several times throughout the day. If he has told her he loves and desires her and if he has aroused her a little and allowed her imagination to do the rest, she has a reason for rejoicing in his arms that evening.

Some people believe that foreplay is exclusively for women's benefit. On the contrary, foreplay provides an opportunity for both husband and wife to enjoy intimately sharing and expressing their love for each other.

Even the animal kingdom enjoys foreplay. Have you ever watched male birds strut around while the females play "hard to get"? Have you ever observed male and female cats snuggle in their own way before mating? Female dogs dance around when in heat. I realize animals don't enjoy love with one another as we do, but they do seem to enjoy demonstrating desire toward each other in their own way.

Foreplay is the same thing. It demonstrates our passions and desires, and it helps us open up to one another emotionally so we can respond physically. The real essence of foreplay is emotional intimacy between two people who love each other and can express their passion in creative ways.

MEN JUST NEED A PLACE

As for men who, according to Billy Crystal, "only need a place," finding creative locations should be no problem. Expand your mind. Don't get into the rut of thinking that a bed is the only suitable place to make love.

Try escaping the privacy of your bedroom and begin to view the rug in front of that roaring fireplace with an altogether new perspective. Invite your wife to meet you under the old elm tree in your backyard.

If you begin playing around with your beloved while driving somewhere, why not just pull over and hop into the backseat? Make love on a thick blanket on the beach, or enjoy intimacy in a boat. Luxuriate in the freedom of an evening in a hotel room. Cuddle up together in a chair and delight in some interesting new positions. Showering together or sharing a Jacuzzi is a great way for intimacy to begin.

While a man may enjoy lovemaking virtually anywhere, a woman may have specific desires regarding the locale. The place for a woman may be quite important. One reason for that is that many women are naturally atmosphere setters, which sensitizes them to the decor and atmosphere in a room. Because women love pleasant surroundings, where they make love will affect them. It can't just be "a place."

For example, a man might not even notice the appearance of his bedroom. However, if his wife doesn't like that room, either unconsciously or consciously it will affect her each time she enters it. Since her feelings greatly influence her ability to enjoy physical intimacy, it is unlikely that she will be satisfied with that part of marriage. In chapter 4, I will further discuss the importance of creating a romantic bedroom atmosphere.

Another thing to remember is that women usually work in the home, even if they work full-time outside the home. Normally, they are still doing some sort of housework after dinner, if only for a short time. Then, later on in the evening, if she is a mother, she is often the one primarily responsible for getting the children into bed. Then she may be getting clothes ready for the next day, packing lunches or doing other work in the home.

When it is finally time for her to retire to the bedroom, her mind may still be on her workplace, home and what has to be done early the next morning. If she and her husband want to engage in physical intimacy, she needs to take off her roles of worker and/or mother and become a lover.

Her emotions are going to need some talking to, some positive influence, before she will be effective in her new role as a lover.

Men, can you imagine making love in your office or place of work when the workflow is hectic? Maybe it wouldn't bother some of you, but it would probably be a struggle for some men to stop work and immediately be in the mood.

CONQUERING AND YIELDING THE LAND

Not only do men and women view environment differently, but they also view sexual intimacy from different perspectives. Conquering is a God-given desire within a man, and he may view intercourse as "conquering the land." Conversely, a woman has the God-given grace to submit, so she may see intercourse as "yielding the land."

Usually armies conquer lands by force and the opposing side doesn't easily surrender. However, in marital intimacy, the "conquering" and "yielding" should be tender, loving, playful and passionate. Force should *never* be an issue.

Furthermore, just because the man is often the more aggressive one, his being "the conqueror" does not necessarily mean that his wife isn't equally eager and aggressive. Often women take the initiative, which men love. Still, one major complaint from married men is that they always have to be the aggressors, or initiators. Just as women want to be wanted, so do men—especially sexually.

If the woman isn't interested, often it is either because she has never been able to show her husband exactly what she desires or her husband skips foreplay and quickly "conquers the land." The husband who ignores his wife's foreplay needs may as well be taking the land by force. If his wife does "yield the land," it is doubtful she does it willingly or passionately. Inwardly, she is fighting all the way, even if outwardly she opens to her husband.

DON'T MISS THE FIRST AND SECOND ACTS

Bringing a great deal of frustration to a woman, intercourse without foreplay is often like beginning a stage play at the final act.

If such intercourse were a play, it might as well be a one-man show, because intercourse without foreplay often means that the leading lady can never fully participate in the show. Instead, she becomes the audience. She watches the final act but wonders how good the first and second acts could have been. When the final bows take place, she feels cheated because she missed out on most of the fun. All the glory and joy of the act go to one person, the actor, while his leading lady sits in the side wings.

For some women, this is all too frequently the case. The reason these women have never been aroused, the reason they are bored with sex and the reason they feign headaches or tiredness is that their husbands are in such a hurry to get to the climax that they forget the first and second acts. Such men need to take another careful look at the script. They need to rediscover the leading lady and find out about her needs. If they'll do this, they might be surprised at the rave reviews they'll receive the next morning.

HOW TO GET RAVE REVIEWS

Men who really want to know how to creatively arouse their wives must realize that emotional feelings and physical touch arouse women. Since men are aroused by sight, a man may be stimulated simply by watching his wife undress. That isn't necessarily so for his wife, however. She may have her mind on something entirely different than sex while she is undressing. Before her husband approaches her sexually, he may need to help her feel romantic, loved and sensual.

It is important for men to realize that women do have to prepare themselves mentally and emotionally for sex. Women aren't as instantly ready as men usually are.

The moment a man shows his wife, whether directly or indirectly, that he desires sexual intimacy, she has a choice to make. She can (1) ignore his approach, (2) resist him, (3) simply succumb to intercourse unwillingly, or (4) choose to make it the best experience she and her husband have ever had.

Just because she isn't "in the mood" doesn't mean she can't get there. And just because she doesn't feel sexy at a particular moment in time doesn't mean she isn't sexy to her husband. Just because it seems that he wants sex more than she does doesn't mean things have to stay that way. In fact, since women are capable of multiple orgasms during intercourse, and the majority of men are not, shouldn't this suggest that God created women to enjoy sex as much as, if not even more than, men?

DEFRAUD YE NOT ONE THE OTHER

Many women's minds just need to be renewed to the truth, especially when it comes to sex. Before a woman can willingly submit to her husband's sexual appetite, especially when at times hers may not be as "hardy" as his, she may need to know what God's Word has to say about it.

In 1 Corinthians 7:1-5 Paul covers this subject well:

> Now concerning the things whereof ye wrote unto me: It is good for a man not to touch a woman. Nevertheless, to avoid fornication, let every man have his own wife, and every woman have her own husband.
>
> Let the husband render unto the wife due benevolence: and likewise also the wife unto the husband. The wife hath not power of her own body, but the husband: and likewise also the husband hath not power of his own body, but the wife.
>
> Defraud ye not one the other, except it be with consent for a time, that ye may give yourselves to fasting and prayer; and come together again, that Satan tempt you not for your incontinency.

Verses 3 through 5 are especially revealing in *The Amplified Version:*

> The husband should give to his wife her conjugal rights—goodwill, kindness and what is due her as his wife; and likewise the wife to her husband.
>
> For the wife does not have [exclusive] authority and control over her own body, but the husband [has his rights]; likewise also the husband does not have [exclusive] authority and control over his body, but the wife [has her rights].

> **Do not refuse and deprive and defraud each other (of your due marital rights), except perhaps by mutual consent for a time, that you may devote yourselves unhindered to prayer. But afterwards resume marital relations, lest Satan tempt you [to sin] through your lack of restraint of sexual desire.**

Did you notice in the above verses that the lack of sexual activity in marriage could lead to sexual sin? This is an area Satan will use to tempt either wives or husbands when sexual intimacy isn't present in their lives. (Please note that there is a difference between sexual *intimacy* and *sex*. In the marriage bed, it is important that each partner shares him- or herself intimately, not just allows the other to have sex with him or her.) If either party is refusing sexual intimacy, this Scripture warns this person that he or she is placing each partner in a precarious position that could lead to sin.

When a husband or wife refuses intimacy with his or her mate, pressure is applied to the marriage. Resistance causes pressure. Pressure must be relieved somehow, in some way, or it can cause explosions.

Have you ever observed a pressure cooker in operation? It must allow steam to escape; otherwise the pressure would cause it to blow up. And what a mess that would make!

Well, that is what happens in a marriage when sexual desires go unfulfilled. There is a blowup somewhere, or else sexual sin takes place, either of which will make for a real mess. It is clear from these verses that it is sin to defraud, or refuse, one's husband or wife of sexual intimacy. Therefore, if sexual fornication takes place because a spouse refuses his or her mate's "due marital rights," both partners are equally in sin and are responsible, regardless of which one actually became involved in an extramarital affair.

This does not, by any means, justify a man's or woman's participation in extramarital sexual activity. Contrarily, a difference in sexual appetites calls for sensitivity, honest communication and mutual compromise between husband and wife.

We Are Not Our Own

In the previous chapter in 1 Corinthians, we can see that Paul is emphasizing a point: We don't belong to ourselves.

> **What? know ye not that your body is the temple of the Holy Ghost which is in you, which ye have of God, and ye are not your own? For ye are bought with a price: therefore glorify God in your body, and in your spirit, which are God's.**
>
> **1 Corinthians 6:19,20**

Our covenant with God makes us His property. Our body is His temple. We are not our own. The precious blood of Jesus bought and paid for us. Fully giving oneself to another is what being in a covenant is all about.

In the marriage covenant, we are not our own. When we marry, we should die to independent living, just as we should when we become the bride of Christ. We can no longer think or live independently of our mates. What we do affects them, just as what we do affects God.

First Corinthians 7:4 clearly states that our bodies are not even our own in marriage. We don't have exclusive control and authority over our own bodies; our mates also have their rights. In other words, if your beloved wants to engage in sexual intimacy with you and you are not in the mood, you should still consent to his or her desires, prepare yourself for intimacy and seek to please your spouse sexually.

The only exception to this is when both parties—not *one* but *both*—decide to set aside time to pray without any distractions, then that is an acceptable reason to mutually refuse sexual pleasures for a time. Sexual desires certainly can be a distraction to prayer. However, it is very clear that these two should resume intimacy afterwards because of Satan's tactics of temptation.

WOMEN, GET READY

With that in mind, women need to learn how to ready themselves for their husbands' advances. And since men's desires start in their thought life, with sight being the arousal point, what can women do to prepare themselves?

It is necessary for a woman to understand that she is a complex creature who is aroused by feelings. Her emotions can be erratic for a variety of reasons: hormonal swings, which cause mood swings; the strain of the day; the pressure of being a mom; the tensions of the workplace. If she comes home to fix dinner, do two loads of laundry, help with the kids' homework, clean up the kitchen and get the kids into bed after a full day, she just may not feel very romantic.

If she has given out all day and her emotions and body are weary, her feelings may be submerged and not easily aroused by her husband's approach. Men, if this is a familiar scene in your home, you need to initiate a change. You may have never thought of it this way, but participating in caring for your home and children is just as much a part of foreplay as are caressing and passionately kissing your beloved.

Even when her husband shares this load, though, a wife may still need to prepare her mind for sexual intimacy. If she knows the Word, she realizes she should yield to her husband's desires, but she first needs to relax. She should sweetly tell him the truth—that she is tired, that she needs time and that she would really appreciate some emotional intimacy first.

Then, she needs to do something to help herself feel ready. Chapter 4 of this book is devoted to instructing women on preparing themselves sexually, but here I will share just a few thoughts.

The quickest and easiest way to wash away the pressures of the day, refresh oneself and feel loving and lovable is to take a warm shower or a soothing bubble bath. In this serenity, a woman can pray and let her cares slip away. God's Word applies regardless of our feelings. Yielding ourselves to our spouses first begins with yielding ourselves to God and His Word.

Next, she could slip into something that makes her feel attractive, sexy or sensual. Providing she has gotten rid of whatever emotional baggage may have been in the way and prayed, asking God to help her and her beloved have an enjoyable, loving experience, she will be ready to enter into sexual foreplay.

Even if a couple have enjoyed an evening of good communication or just had fun together, a woman will most likely still need time to prepare.

BUILD UP SLOWLY TO THE CLIMAX

Not only does it take a woman more time to prepare for sexual intimacy, but it also takes her more time to reach a climax. If a man lacks control, he may peak and finish intercourse very quickly. But women slowly peak, slowly reach an orgasm, or multiple orgasms, and continue the sensations for several minutes after intercourse has subsided. She enjoys an "afterglow" and usually wants to talk, while her husband feels tired and ready to sleep.

The longer the foreplay, the greater the climax for both men and women. So enjoy it, knowing you will both benefit from the fun.

God designed the following events that occur naturally during foreplay, so that sexual intercourse can be extremely enjoyable for both a husband and his wife.

During foreplay, a man achieves an erection as blood flows into his penis.

As her clitoris is stimulated it becomes enlarged and bright red in color. When her clitoris is enlarged, it is even more sensitive, and this makes orgasm possible for the woman.

If the woman is being aroused successfully, her vagina is secreting a natural lubricant and her vaginal walls are contracting. If a woman isn't lubricated, intercourse will be painful. Lubricants are available on the market to assist a woman's body in this effort.

When a woman's vaginal muscles have contracted and thickened, penetration will be much more pleasurable for both her and her husband.

God really knew what He was doing when He designed human bodies. Foreplay brings pleasure emotionally, physically and even spiritually.

The Shulamite told Solomon exactly what she wanted. We certainly ought to do the same. If we don't, we are left to arousal assumptions, which only lead to intimate dissolution and sad sex.

CHAPTER 4

Wake Up, Women!

I sleep, but my heart waketh: it is the voice of my beloved that knocketh, saying, Open to me, my sister, my love, my dove, my undefiled: for my head is filled with dew, and my locks with the drops of the night.

Song of Solomon 5:2

God's Word admonishes us to think on things that are good. (Phil. 4:8.) Sex is good, and we need to think on that until it is a truth that is settled in our hearts.

Sex is honorable in marriage. It is beneficial to our spirits, souls and bodies. It brings unity and harmony between two married people as no other natural act can. It assures each partner of the other's love and of God's great love for us. It brings us a sense of well-being and nourishes our hearts. It is a powerful tool against the enemy's tactics and diffuses his explosive missiles sent to destroy our marriages. *Think on these things.*

Women need to guard their minds against the indifference toward sex. It can so easily sneak up on them, especially if they aren't feeling fulfilled sexually or in other ways. In the book *Solomon on Sex,* a letter written in jest exposes how a woman's indifference toward sex can affect a man. It begins:

To my loving wife:

During the past year I have tried to make love to you 365 times. I have succeeded only thirty-six times; this is an average of once every ten days. The following is a list of why I did not succeed more often:

It will wake the children ....27 times

It's too late ....23 times

It's too hot ....16 times

It's too cold ....5 times

It's too early ....15 times

Pretended to be asleep...............................46 times

Windows open, neighbors will hear ....9 times

Backache ....26 times

Headache ....18 times

Toothache ....13 times

Giggles ....6 times

Not in the mood ....36 times

Too full ....10 times

Baby is crying ....17 times

Watched late TV show ....17 times

I watched late TV show ....15 times

Company in next room ....11 times

You had to go to the bathroom ....19 times

TOTAL ....329 times

During the thirty-six times I did succeed, the activity was not entirely satisfactory due to the following:

1. Six times you chewed gum the whole time.
2. Seven times you watched TV the whole time.
3. Sixteen times you told me to hurry up and get it over with.
4. Six times I tried to wake you to tell you we were through.
5. One time I was afraid I had hurt you, for I felt you move.

Honey, it's no wonder I'm so irritable.

Your Loving Husband[1]

While the above material was written in jest, does any of it ring a bell? If so, have you asked yourself why?

Why isn't your joy full in this area? What can you do to change that? Most women have full schedules each day. They don't have the high levels of testosterone that their counterparts do to remind them as frequently of sex. Many women have children, homes and outside jobs to keep them preoccupied. Often, by the time they fall into bed, the last thing on their minds is ministering to their husbands' desires.

Since the most important sex organ is the mind, each partner must turn his or her mind off the daily drudges—what needs to be done tomorrow, what wasn't accomplished today, why the kids aren't doing so well in school, why the boss is so edgy, how to pay the bills next payday and how to manage to feed the family. Only then will each be able to minister to the other's needs.

Ministering is what sexual intercourse between husband and wife is all about. It is ministry, serving each other in a very physical, intimate way.

UNDERSTAND HINDRANCES TO SEXUAL FULFILLMENT

Before I go into the things that you can do to promote this ministry, I want you to know that there are several significant hindrances to a woman's ability to enjoy sexual intimacy with her husband. As you read on, you may identify with some of these. Remember that God wants you to be fulfilled in your marriage, so if there *are* hindrances, you can make them a matter of prayer, take the practical steps I've mentioned to deal with them and believe for an abundant sexual relationship with your husband.

Caring for a Newborn

If you are a new mom with a small baby, you may be too occupied in ministering to your infant's needs, especially during those first few months, to desire physical intimacy with your husband. Sometimes continual caregiving can be quite consuming, and you may simply be too tired or emotionally drained to think beyond your own needs even when the little one is finally asleep.

This, however, is a time when you need to be especially careful and diligent to minister to your husband's needs too. When you minister to him sexually, you are receiving as well, and you need the relaxation and other benefits that satisfying sexual intimacy provide just as much as he does.

Fear of Pregnancy

Possibly, you simply don't want to get pregnant again. If this is the case, be sure that you and your husband have agreed on some type of birth control. This will ease your mind and help you enjoy the experience.

God has given us authority over our bodies and told us to take dominion over the earth. Through various forms of birth control, we have been provided a way to prevent conceiving more children than we can effectively rear. Therefore, it may be wise to look into them, discuss them with your spouse and decide which method will be best for you.

If you choose to use the rhythm method, abstinence during the seven-day period of fertility, then abstinence should not extend longer than the seven-day period agreed upon by the couple to be used as a time of prayer. If it does, then the reasons for the abstinence need to be examined.

Unfortunately, some people are raised with the idea that sex is only for procreation. Animals engage in intercourse only when they are in heat. However, we are not animals; sex for married couples is intended for much more than procreation. It is intended for pleasure as well and can and should be enjoyed during infertile periods as well.

If one spouse or the other should insist on having sex only for the purpose of procreation, then this will cause great frustration. Such thinking is contrary to God's nature.

Yes, He is a God of reproduction and planned that everything would reproduce after its kind. And, yes, children truly are, just as Psalm 127:3-5 says, a heritage of the Lord and whoever has his quiver full of them will be tremendously blessed. Yet the beauty of procreation is not the only reason God designed sexual intimacy.

Some of the teachings that promote extreme forms of abstinence will use the Scripture in Genesis 38:9-10, where a man named Onan sinned by spilling his semen, or seed, on the ground rather than producing a child for his deceased brother. The idea they bring out here is that the semen, or seed, should be used for the purpose of procreation only and is not to be interrupted or destroyed along the way.

But if you read the context of that passage, you will see that God was displeased by the motive of Onan's heart, not the action of spilling his semen.

The custom then was for the next oldest brother of the one who had died to marry his brother's widow and give her a son if there was none, so his name could be carried on. In this case, Onan, wanting the son to be his own, rebelled by spilling his semen on the ground, lest he should give his seed to his brother. His selfishness angered God, and Onan died because of the motive behind the action of spilling the seed, not the spilling of the seed.

I see nothing in the Scriptures indicating that God prohibits the use of various birth control methods or that sex is only for procreation. However, I advise you to search out the Scriptures for yourselves and to seek God's counsel as a couple about your approach.

Sexual Victimization

Probably the greatest hindrance to sexual fulfillment is the memory—whether it be repressed or conscious—of sexual abuse. Whether it happened during childhood or later in life, the memories can linger and cause a woman to devalue her own and/or her husband's sexuality. Studies show that one-third of all women have been sexually molestated. Those figures are staggering and make us aware of just how many women have been affected by this kind of pain.

A few years ago I counseled a young wife who explained that she had experienced an orgasm just once on her honeymoon, but since then, sex had been frustrating and not enjoyable for her. Her husband had great concern for her, and, of course, his own ego was affected because he was unable to satisfy her needs in this area.

She felt her home life had a great effect on her inability to release herself in sex. Her mother never taught her anything about being a woman, and her dad abandoned her at a young age. Emotionally, her mother abandoned her too. While such a poor example would certainly affect a sexual relationship negatively, the Holy Spirit led me to ask her if she'd had any bad sexual relationships. She briefly revealed a date rape situation to me.

I then went on to explain the spiritual ramifications of sexual abuse. The Bible tells us that when a man joins himself to a harlot the two become one body. (1 Cor. 6:16.) The sexual bond is not only physical but is emotional and spiritual as well. Whatever spirit is attached to one person will transfer to his or her sexual partner. Sometimes lustful spirits or even perverted spirits are transferred through the one-flesh act.

I believe this transferring of spirits may be one of the reasons that some women are repeatedly raped. When a girl is first sexually molested, lustful spirits attach themselves to her. Then other men, who are harassed by those same spirits, are drawn to her. Often familiar spirits are involved, and sometimes they are there because of generational sins and curses.

Unfortunately, the court systems have often blamed such women, but she is the innocent one. Sometimes she is blamed for dressing in an alluring manner, but the truth is that she doesn't have to dress sexually to attract men. Those spirits will attract them.

After explaining this to this young woman, we prayed and took authority over any spirits that might have attached themselves to her because of that situation and commanded them to leave in Jesus' name. Even though after the incident she'd had no desire to ever see the man who had made her the victim of date rape, she broke any soul ties with him by vocally renouncing any desires of her heart toward him.

I might add that I also prayed for wonderfully fulfilling intercourse for both her and her husband. For a woman who has been sexually molested, the biggest challenge in life may be to trust men, especially if the molestation was repeated and if her father or an authority figure was the aggressor. She may have developed a deep-seated hatred for men as a result.

It takes forgiveness, the God-kind of forgiveness, and the use of your authority in the name of Jesus to start the process of deliverance.

During our marriage seminars, Glenn and I often pray for women who have been molested. We find that women who first make the choice to forgive those who molested them can be set totally free. Then we expect the anointing to do the rest. When we lay hands on them, we take authority over all of the spirits involved. We pray for the restoration of their uniqueness as women, for that sense of purity to return and for the healing process to be completed.

For this young wife whom I counseled, the outcome was astounding. She later told me in detail the results of that counseling and prayer session. She said she was now completely free and enjoyed sexual intimacy with her husband again and was experiencing orgasms each time.

You can take these steps toward freedom in the privacy of your own home if you totally understand your authority and what is taking place spiritually. As a believer, you have an anointing within you to help you process all that is needed for freedom.

More often than not, forgiveness and anointed prayer bring about total deliverance, but there are also times when a woman has been so emotionally bruised that she needs further counseling. You may need the help of another if you feel your emotional damage is beyond your own prayer ability. In that case, I strongly advise you to talk with your pastor or a recommended counselor who can help you.

Disrespect for Men

Several years ago a young mother called me for counseling. She had been in one of our marriage seminars but had not attended the session on sex and was having difficulty with her sex life. When she married her husband their love was great, but she was unable to achieve an orgasm.

As we spoke, I mentioned other possible reasons for a woman's inability to have an orgasm. She quickly identified the problem: Her mother had planted in her young mind seeds of disrespect and distrust toward men. Her father had left home when she was very young. She hadn't been aware of the depth of the disrespect until the Holy Spirit revealed it as we talked. Those seeds had grown inside of her, and she had no respect for men in general, and subconsciously, she lacked respect for her husband specifically.

So over the phone we prayed for her and her difficulty in respecting men. She knew the Word of God quite well and knew how to operate in faith. I referred her to Ephesians 5:33 which speaks of wives respecting their husbands. *The Amplified Version* puts it this way:

> **However, let each man of you (without exception) love his wife as [being in a sense] his very own self; and let the wife see that she respects and reverences her husband—that she notices him, regards him, honors him, prefers him, venerates and esteems him; and that she defers to him, praises him, and loves and admires him exceedingly.**

Just a few days after our phone conversation, I received a letter from this woman. She had renounced all disrespect for men. That very day she had put her little ones down for a nap and sat down with the Word of God and began to confess that she loved and respected her husband. She meditated on that Scripture all day, and that night during lovemaking with her husband she achieved an orgasm. She was so grateful to God for what He had done in such a short time.

Truly He is a God of total deliverance.

Failure To Submit

Respect and submission go hand in hand in marriage. God admonishes all believers to submit to one another and to treat each other as better than themselves.

Submission, just like respect, is an attitude of the heart. However, a wife's actions will certainly reveal the attitudes of her heart. A woman who outwardly controls her husband lacks respect for him and does not submit to him in her heart. Such women are often very controlling people, and they try to take over their husbands' positions of leadership in their homes.

Ephesians 5:22 says, **Wives, submit yourselves unto your own husbands, as unto the Lord**. When a woman disobeys this command, she will not be blessed. Isaiah 1:19 says, **If ye be willing and obedient, ye shall eat the good of the land.**

A wife who does not experience orgasms in sexual intimacy with her husband does not partake of the "good of the land." She suffers lack in the one area where God has supplied so many special benefits for women.

In chapter 1, I referred to a woman's need to feel loved and secure in that love, to feel absolute safety and trust so that she can "let go" and climax. When she does this, she "yields the land" to her husband not only physically but also emotionally. If she does not or cannot yield emotionally, she won't climax physically.

Some women don't submit to or respect their husbands because they are ignorant of God's Word. But once you have been enlightened to the Word, specifically the passage in Ephesians 5:21-33, it is up to you to change your mind and do the Word.

This may take time, but remember, we are talking about changing an attitude, not simply actions. If God can change Pharaoh's hardened heart, He can change the attitude of a woman's heart. But it is up to her to submit herself to the will and Word of God.

Unfortunately most women who are not submissive to their husbands are also not submissive to God. Since the condition of our submission as wives is as unto the Lord (Eph. 5:22), it is impossible to submit to your husband without submitting to the Lord.

We have already read one example of a woman who simply believed God and His Word rather than her learned attitudes toward men. Her disrespect wasn't completely her fault. Her mother had planted it in her. If she hadn't responded positively to the Word and the Spirit of God, she wouldn't have experienced the "good of the land" that night with her husband.

Women, the choice is yours. Either you do the Word and are blessed, or you disobey and suffer lack. And suffering lack in physical intimacy with your husband is too precious, too vital to your well-being and to your marriage, for you to take that risk.

Healthy bodies come from healthy relationships, first with God and then with others. We have shown how sex can even bring health in some areas of our bodies. We have seen how an orgasm brings relaxation and restoration to our bodies. We have seen how a climax brings a sense of oneness and unity, as well as how it releases tension and calms nerves. Your health is wrapped up in a good sex life with your husband. Intimacy and the sexual union that brings intimacy to a culmination are too important to risk by failing to submit to God and to your husband.

So, ladies, if submission and respect are difficult for you, I admonish you to deal with those areas scripturally. For a better understanding of those two areas, I encourage you to study the Word of God and then read Pat Harrison's book, *Woman, Wife, Mother.*[2]

There is no better formula for a successful marriage than what is found in Scripture.

A WORD OF CAUTION ABOUT SUBMISSION

Respect for one's husband is certainly a necessary element in the formula for marital success. However, some abusive husbands use Scripture to support their abuse. *This is a misuse of Scripture and is not at all what God intended.* Unfortunately, these husbands are not taking into account the whole counsel of God, which calls *every* Christian into submission to every other Christian and admonishes the husband to love his wife protectively and sacrificially just as Christ loved the Church. (Eph. 5:21,25.)

If you find yourself in a situation such as this, I would suggest that you no longer suffer in silence but that you find a qualified counselor in whom you can trust and begin to take whatever the necessary steps are to bring the relationship back into balance.

PREPARE FOR THE BEST

Now that we've covered some of the hindrances of a woman's ability to enjoy sexual intimacy, let's look at what she can do to prepare herself for the best sexual encounters with her husband, time and time again. Following is a list from the heart and from a wide variety of people and experiences.

TAKE A BUBBLE BATH

As I mentioned earlier, one of the best ways to unwind each evening is to take a bubble bath. Fill the tub with lots of warm water and fragrant bubbles. Allow all the cares of the day and the concerns of your heart to vanish in those warm bubbles. Cast every care on the Lord and begin to concentrate on your husband, on how much you love and appreciate him. Begin to think romantic thoughts about him and even bring to mind your great times in bed.

When your body has sufficiently relaxed and your mind is far from anything that would hinder lovemaking and is instead filled with things that will enhance it, you are ready to get out of the tub. You could powder yourself with beautiful talc or apply your favorite lotion or perfume. Then put on something that makes you feel romantic and sexy.

THE POWER OF SEXY LINGERIE

Many women have inaccurately been told, or have felt, that sexy lingerie is inappropriate for Christians. That is absolute hogwash. Why should the sinners have all the fun in the act of marriage, which God ordained?

Many women think, again inaccurately, that sexy garments are for their husbands. I present to you this question: Who feels sexy and romantic when she wears lingerie?

The truth is that sexy garments, even undergarments, will help you feel sexy and romantic. Lacy bras and panties are a reminder of your femininity and sexual appeal. If you will make a small investment in such items, you will be sure to feel prettier and more attractive.

And while I'm on the subject, please be aware that your husband most likely does not like seeing you in holey undergarments. Your being well dressed, even down to your undergarments, is a reflection of his ability to take good care of you. Make sure to pitch out those old things. If necessary, believe God for nice, new ones.

READ A GOOD BOOK ON SEX

Besides preparing yourself with a nice long bubble bath and romantic garments, one really good way to prepare yourself for a blissful, intimate experience with your husband is to read a good book on sex. Tim and Beverly LaHaye's *The Act of Marriage* is one of the many good Christian books on marital sex that can be found at your local Christian bookstore or possibly even in your church library.[3]

Watching romantic movies or thinking romantic thoughts will also help you prepare your mind for sexual intimacy with your beloved.

CREATE A ROMANTIC ATMOSPHERE IN YOUR BEDROOM

Believe it or not, your bedroom is probably one of the greatest assets for helping you get in the mood. If possible, go into your bedroom right now; otherwise, just think about it for a minute. Now, ask yourself, "Would

Hollywood choose this room for a romantic scene?" If the answer is no, then look around and mentally eliminate those articles that are unromantic or unappealing to your eyes.

How do you think such items affect you when you walk into your bedroom? It may be unconscious, but it does affect you adversely.

For example, suppose an ironing board is standing in the corner stacked with yesterday's—or worse yet, last week's—laundry. Your mind will remember all you need to do to get that laundry ironed and put away.

Suppose in one corner stands a desk filled with work to be done, bills to be paid and clutter. Suppose your room is so messy and cluttered that it looks like a hurricane hit it? Your mind will think about tending to everything but your husband.

Suppose your bedroom decor appeals to your husband's manly taste but doesn't reflect your personality. You will think of things that are unappealing and unromantic.

If your bedroom is not an appealing, restful haven, your mind will be bogged down with things that are not good, not lovely, not of good report, and certainly not sexually passionate in nature each time you walk in the door.

If you carefully read the Song of Solomon, you will find that Solomon used the finest wool and tapestry to decorate his bridal chamber. It was a beautiful sanctuary for their love. The Shulamite came into his palace, so he decorated it for her.

If your bedroom is not a beautiful sanctuary for your love, then you need to change it or add romantic things to it for your own benefit. Though the room itself probably won't directly affect your husband, he will be pleased by your newfound comfort and emotional freedom to enjoy his intimate embrace.

I remember one young pastor's wife taking me into her bedroom when we were staying with her and her husband. She said, "I hate my bedroom. No wonder I'm not interested in sex anymore." We found just a few changes she could make that were quick, effective and inexpensive.

Candles, soft music and flowers, along with a few little frills, can make such a difference to a room. Nice sheets, new bedspreads and drapes can change a bedroom dramatically.

You don't need to do it all at once. Just begin by cleaning up any obvious work spaces and adding a few romantic touches. Your bedroom should be as beautiful as will fit your budget and decorating desires.

MAKE ADVANCES TOWARD YOUR HUSBAND

If you read the Song of Solomon, you will notice that the Shulamite not only enjoyed her husband's advances but also pursued him sexually.

For some women, this is not easy. Many have been taught that men pursue women, not vice versa.

While men are often the ones told to never stop chasing their wives, that doesn't mean women can't have some fun and do a little pursuing too. In fact, many men love being chased. They want to feel wanted.

One of my daughters told me about a friend of hers who likes to surprise her husband. One day she arranged to meet him for lunch. When he walked out to the car, she had on a coat with nothing under it. Can you imagine his surprise as he got into that car and she unwrapped that coat?

You don't have to go to this extreme measure, but think of ways to show your husband how much you desire him. It will be worth your effort.

PLAN A WEEKEND GETAWAY

Recently Glenn and I went away for a weekend trip to a cozy little place in southern Oklahoma, near Turner Falls. Our room had a fireplace and paneled walls and a view of the rapids from the back windows, which we opened to hear that wonderful bubbling sound.

It had been an especially tiring week for Glenn, so I wasn't expecting any big romantic evening. I had purchased some massage lotion for the trip, so I offered to give Glenn a massage.

Before I got started, I put on one of his favorite Christian jazz tapes, lit a wonderfully scented candle, turned off all the lights and began his massage. As he began to relax, I told him to just receive and that I wasn't expecting anything in return because I just wanted to soothe his weary body.

Well, you probably already guessed the end result. But my heart was really just to bless Glenn. I knew he needed to get away, and all that mattered to me was just that he could relax.

The next night he gave me a massage, and the entire weekend turned out to be wonderfully relaxing and very romantic.

May I suggest that you arrange a time away for just the two of you? It will do your marriage good. Just a motel date overnight would do wonders. How about just making the plans and announcing to him that the two of you are going away for a "second honeymoon?"

How To Promote Romance

Speaking of honeymoons, do you remember yours? How did you prepare yourself for it? Did you buy a wonderfully feminine and romantic outfit for that first night?

If you want the romance of your honeymoon to return, what are you doing to promote it?

Do you know how to please your husband sexually? Do you know what turns him on, where his sensitive spots are, what he likes you to do to him?

Do you look attractive to him when he comes home? Do you wear makeup and fix your hair just for him? Or do you fix yourself up only for work, church or other times when you leave the house?

Do you build him up and encourage him? Or do you nag him, make him feel like a heel and criticize him?

Are your words toward him full of praise? Do you whisper suggestive ideas in his ears and make him feel very appealing? Maybe suggestive talking just isn't your bag, but you need to find some way of letting him know you want him.

What about just placing your hand on his thigh while you are dining in a restaurant? (Make sure there is a tablecloth hiding your actions, of course.) Or what about entering the bathroom while he is shaving in his shorts and running your fingers up his legs? What about writing a little note to him or sending him suggestive cards?

If your husband has a personal phone at work, how about calling him someday and telling him, "Honey, I can't wait till you get home tonight?"

I think by now you have the idea: Make your husband feel sexy and romantic in whatever way you can. Build up his ego, rather than tearing it down. Dress up in your finest for him, especially at night when you are going to bed.

HAVING DONE ALL, PRAY

Perhaps you have done all of the above and you still need help. Call on God and pray—over yourself and your bed. A good Scripture for encouragement is Genesis 18:12 NKJV, where Sarah said, **After I have grown old, shall I have pleasure, my lord being old also?** God had just spoken that she would have a child, and she knew the action involved in making her pregnant was going to bring her pleasure.

RECLAIM YOUR ROLE

In chapter 3, I compared lovemaking to a play. If you've felt like that leading lady who has lost her role and has been sitting on the sidelines, it's time to reclaim your role. Here are some ways you can better enjoy playing your part.

During foreplay, don't be inactive. Just like you, your husband has arousal spots; find them and caress him. If you feel he's responding too quickly, caress him very slowly.

Let him know what pleases you. Respond to him in words and actions. Be open to trying new positions and finding different arousal points.

Do Kegel exercises to make your vagina more sensitive and muscles more responsive. *Intended for Pleasure* is a good book to instruct you on these if needed.[4]

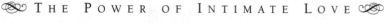

Then be sure to keep your mind on what you are doing. Yield yourself to him—body and soul. Love him and his body with all that is within you. Picture yourself really letting go and releasing your all to him.

IT'S ALL ABOUT LOVE

Keep in mind that skill and sexual technique are not the most important issues here. Relationship and expressing your love for one another are what sexual intercourse is all about.

Depending upon your needs, the time of your monthly cycle and your hormonal and energy levels, your sexual experiences could widely differ. One time it may seem exceedingly exotic; another time it may be simply sweet; still another time it could be wonderfully wild.

Regardless, what matters is that your love for one another is being expressed intimately and fully. If that is taking place, God is well pleased and you should be too.

CHAPTER 5

Miserably Mistaken Men

A bundle of myrrh is my wellbeloved unto me;
he shall lie all night betwixt my breasts.
Song of Solomon 1:13

Whoever said "ignorance is bliss" was mistaken. In the marriage bed, ignorance is miserable and often ends up in mistakes. I am constantly surprised at the number of men in this generation who are ignorant about their wives' sexual anatomy and how to arouse them.

That's why I've written this chapter, addressed specifically to you men who want to satisfy your wives.

THE WOMAN COMPLEX

Every husband needs to keep in mind the complexity of his female counterpart when trying to build a fire that will burn throughout their marriage. Women are sometimes fragile, supersensitive creatures whose buttons can't easily be pushed, whose emotions are often erratic, whose hormones fluctuate drastically and whose desires change daily.

I have already stated that women are aroused differently than men. Men, who are aroused by sight and who have higher testosterone levels, don't need a lot to heat them up. But women, who are aroused by feelings and touch and whose hormone levels continually change and alter her feelings and desires, need constant affirmation to keep those emotions in line. Emotional affirmations don't always need to come from a woman's husband, but it certainly helps when they do.

KEEP YOUR SPEECH SWEET

In the Song of Solomon 5:16, the Shulamite sums up her husband's description with these words:

> **His mouth is most sweet: yea, he is altogether lovely. This is my beloved, and this is my friend, O daughters of Jerusalem.**

While she spent several preceding sentences hailing Solomon's great body—mentioning his hair, eyes, cheeks, lips, hands, belly and legs—her summation is most revealing. She speaks of his mouth being sweet, but she wasn't talking about his great-tasting toothpaste or mouthwash. She was referring to the tender, loving speech that came out of his mouth.[1] In her eyes, he is altogether lovely, her beloved, her friend, because he speaks sweet, tender words to her.

"This is my friend," the Shulamite affectionately says. Friends don't speak unkindly about one another and remain friends very long. Friends communicate on a very personal level. Friends stay with each other through thick and thin. Friends lay down their lives for each other. (John 15:13.) Love is the basis of friendship. Friends know how to help you when you hurt, how to minister to your needs when you need encouragement, how to help you stand when you think you are about to fall, how to build you up instead of pushing you down. Friends are beloved.

Far too many married couples have never cultivated the friendship factor in their relationships. Perhaps you and your spouse spent so much of your courtship cultivating your physical intimacy that you never really cultivated your friendship.

It took several years of marriage before Glenn and I even recognized that the essential friendship factor was missing from our marriage.

Glenn spent the first ten years of our marriage attending night college while working fifty to sixty hours per week. He crammed studying for his difficult engineering classes between classroom hours and weekends. Our kids rarely spent time with their father, except for the two and a half summer months each year.

On top of all this, Glenn had a severe drinking problem due to emotional wounds suffered during childhood. So he often skipped dinner and school and drank the night away for the first ten years of our marriage. Needless to say, none of these facts led to a happy marriage, much less a friendly one. I certainly didn't feel like he was "my beloved."

But in spite of all this, he was always a good lover. He always knew how to "turn me on," and because I loved him so much and was extremely committed to marriage, our sexual relationship was good—not great, but good.

Then, as we became good friends and enjoyed each other's fellowship, it got even better.

One reason our sex life was so good was that Glenn's speech was always "sweet." Glenn, who is a very vocal person, was always complimentary about my looks and my abilities as a homemaker and a mother. He always raved that he had the best wife in the world and bragged about me to his co-workers.

Glenn told me he loved me several times a day. He still does. Sometimes he will make my day by calling and leaving a tender, sweet and touching message on our answering machine.

This kind of thoughtfulness and attention to your wife's emotional needs could bring a whole new dimension of friendship and love into your marriage. And hearing your spoken expressions of love could be just what your wife needs to feel truly free in her expression of love for you in physical intimacy.

TENDER SPEECH IS NOT ENOUGH

But tender speech alone won't do it. If you were just a great friend, but were insensitive to your wife's sexual needs and desires, those sweet words and that great friendship wouldn't be enough to arouse her.

Though technique alone won't cause a woman's temperature to rise, you do have to know how to find your wife's anatomical turn-on button.

That "button" is known as the clitoris. Some men mistakenly think the vagina is where their wives need stimulation, but they are mistaken. Stimulating the vagina may be somewhat pleasurable, but stimulating the clitoris is essential to orgasm.

The clitoris and the penis are similar in their sensitivity and function. They both require arousal for climax. In fact, before the male organs form in a fetus, the clitoris is in place. Then, from the clitoris, the male's testicles and penis develop.

A common complaint from women is that men think they need to stroke or rub the vagina to stimulate it. Actually, they need to caress the clitoris instead.

And notice, I did not say massage it; I said caress it. Massaging the clitoris can cause discomfort. Always keep in mind the tenderness of the female body. The lighter the touch, the better, especially in the beginning stages of foreplay. Few women ever want rough sex play. Some may like a little firmer stroking later on, but not at first.

The clitoris can be caressed, manually or orally, according to her and your preference, but it is important to remember that continual caressing causes further arousal. Be careful not to interrupt stimulation by moving away too soon. Slowly moving up and down the clitoris as well as the lips of the vagina, or caressing the clitoris and the breasts simultaneously, is extremely effective for most women.

If your wife isn't the type to be vocal about what excites her, you will need to be observant of her breathing patterns and the way her body responds to your caresses. As the clitoris becomes aroused, it enlarges and turns a bright pink.

A woman's breasts are very sensitive and usually respond to gentle caresses and kisses. In fact, her neck and entire chest will respond to light stroking. Bypassing the breast and neck areas for the vagina and clitoris can turn a woman off rather than on, especially if you go straight to her vagina. Internal stimulation of the vagina too early in foreplay will definitely slow down the process and probably irritate your wife.

Hurrying foreplay will only defeat the purpose of it. The longer the foreplay, the greater the climax for both of you, so why rush things? Tease her by caressing, stroking and kissing her until her temperature rises to the point that she can't wait for you to come into her.

As both partners caress one another's bodies and express their love to each other in many ways, they will be aroused by the acts of both giving and receiving.

PLEASE YOUR WIFE FIRST

In the Song of Solomon 1:13, the Shulamite says, **A bundle of myrrh is my wellbeloved unto me; he shall lie all night betwixt my breasts.** Myrrh was an expensive fragrance, so apparently Solomon smelled good and used the best aftershave and cologne he could afford.

There is a simple lesson in this Scripture: Women like men who smell good. If you want to "lie all night betwixt her breasts," you had better smell good.

The Shulamite enjoyed the presence of her beloved between her breasts all night, not only because he smelled good but because he loved her and she was secure in his love and trusted his ability to arouse her and to bring her to an exhilarating climax.

Unfortunately, some men ignore the sensual foreplay women need and want and selfishly press for instant gratification. The result? They eliminate the very thing they are hoping to accomplish.

The Jews had an old saying stating that a man should never accomplish his climax before his wife did. He was to wait until she first had an orgasm to have his.

Of course, the ideal situation would be for both partners to climax at the same time. Certainly this would be mutually satisfying and create great excitement.

Some men think they can't, or simply don't want to, wait until their wives come to that point, but when husbands exhibit more interest in pleasing their wives than themselves, they become the best lovers. This is actually the basis of agape love—loving the other without expecting anything in return. Of course we know if a man arouses his wife, he will receive something in return. But if his aim is to please her first, then agape love is at work. And any man who operates in this kind of love never fails. (See 1 Cor. 13:8.)

When a woman is ready to receive her man, she has a sense of losing all control, so trust is essential for her to allow herself to climax. Many women who seem frigid are not in actuality frigid at all. They just can't, for whatever reason, trust a man enough to "let go."

Trust includes knowing her mate will wait until she is ready to receive him. There is great comfort in that. She will feel cheated; indeed, she is being cheated if she is not aroused to the point of orgasm. If a woman is almost there and her husband enters too soon, she may become very frustrated, which could cause her body to stop responding. She could be turned off immediately and lose interest in intercourse.

Imagine what it would be like to be almost totally aroused only to have something "shut down" inside of you and all desire suddenly leave your body. Keep that in mind before you enter into the final phases of intercourse. Be sure your wife is really ready.

PRAY ABOUT YOUR SEX LIFE

If you are concerned about your ability to maintain an erection, many books suggest helpful practical exercises and ideas, but prayer is essential. If your desire is to please your wife and she is taking longer than you planned or than you think you can maintain an erection, then pray. Ask God to help you be exactly what she needs and to help you arouse her to that perfect place while you maintain your own erection. Some have not, because they ask not. (James 4:2.)

You might balk at the idea of praying about your sex life, but few women would. In fact, many wives are praying that their husbands would learn some things about their sexual needs.

If you would simply listen to the Holy Spirit and make love to your wife according to His direction, she would be well satisfied and so would you. Who would better know what a woman needs than the Holy Spirit, who was there when woman was created. In fact, the Holy Spirit is the One who brings about the action of God's spoken words. He knows a woman's every need and desire, her moods, her emotional well-being, her body's arousal points, her hormone levels and her heart. Sometimes women don't have a total understanding of their needs from day to day, but the Holy Spirit does. And He is a teacher, the best possible instructor one could have. He can teach husbands how to make love to their wives and vice versa if we will simply ask for His help.

Some men wouldn't think of asking for directions when they are lost somewhere on the highway, so they might not be comfortable asking for sexual instructions either. But I urge you to put your ego aside and get the help you need. Read some good books that deal with the subject too.

DON'T JUST GO FOR THE GOLD

One thing about God is that He is very practical as well as spiritual. When He created the male species, He placed practicality, logic and goal orientation within them. However, reaching goals is not what sex is all about.

In *Real Moments for Lovers,* a wonderful little book filled with wisdom about true lovers, popular secular author and speaker Barbara DeAngelis says:

> When sex is about reaching a goal, you will miss out on the moments that could transform it into true lovemaking. You will be too busy trying to turn your partner on, or trying to have an orgasm, or trying to make your sexual encounter match some fantasy picture you have in your head of how sex "should" be. You're focused on what you want to happen, so you can't fully experience what is happening.[2]

That is a vital truth we all—men and women alike—must remember. Either a man or a woman could be so goal oriented that he or she could miss the forest for the trees.

Just "going for the gold," so to speak, will prevent you from enjoying the trip there. I wonder how many of the pioneers enjoyed the countryside while traveling into frontiers unknown.

Were they thinking exclusively about the gold at the end of that rainbow, or did they notice the beauty of the majestic mountain peaks and steep canyons along the way? Did they look beyond the dusty trail to see the delicate flowers on a cactus plant or the wild beauty of a rapidly flowing river nearby?

There is beauty to behold in lovemaking, and God designed your wife's body for you to behold with your eyes, with your hands and with your lips. It wasn't simply designed so that you could enjoy a climax. It wasn't even designed so that you could bring *her* to a climax. Her body was designed for love—to be the bearer of her love and the receiver of your love.

So if being a creative lover requires some time, some prayer and some thoughtful pursuit, enjoy every moment of that time and every color of your mutual love, rather than just going for the end result.

THE GREAT ROMANCER

Consider for a moment your relationship with God. Did you know He is thinking of you and that you are continually on His mind? The psalmist says that His thoughts toward you are greater in number than the sand.

(Ps. 139:17,18.) Because He desires intimate fellowship with you, He is continually wooing you to be with Him. Wooing you takes God's thoughtful time and patience. He knows you aren't always ready to receive His love, so He uses creative ways to show you how much you mean to Him.

He takes the time to know you individually. He knows what you like and what you don't like. He knows how to communicate specifically with you so that you understand, and He is always there for you and ready to listen to you day or night. I'm sure He isn't bored, or boring, nor does He ever force you to do anything against your will. He is a gentleman in every sense of the word, and He is constantly making sure you know He loves you in one way or another. Yes, His romance is spiritual in nature, but the principles are much the same as the romance your marriage needs.

Romance means different things to different people. When you think of romance between a husband and wife, what picture comes to your mind? Now what if I were to ask your wife that same question? What picture do you think would come to her mind? Her picture is probably much different from yours.

Do you remember how you once romanced your sweetie before you married her? You most likely showered and shaved before picking her up for a date. You probably asked her earlier in the week, or at least earlier that day, where she would like to go and gave her plenty of time to be prepared—her hair done just right and her clothes appropriate for wherever you were taking her. If you were planning to dine together, you selected a place that had a romantic atmosphere—soft music, dimmed lights, flowers on each table, fine china and crystal stemware. It wasn't the Golden Arches.

Maybe you even bought her a bouquet of flowers or a corsage. On some special occasion or just because you loved her, you probably brought her some small token of your love—a piece of jewelry, a card, a stuffed animal or candy.

If you drove her somewhere, you probably took those corners a little wildly so she would end up on your side, really close to you. Then you would put your arm around her and drive with one hand. You would sneak in a kiss anytime you could manage it—at stoplights and even while you were driving. You would help her out of the car and take her arm as you escorted her into the restaurant.

Once inside the restaurant, you would help her remove her coat, check it for her and ask for the best table in the house. You probably even insisted on holding her chair for her while she was being seated.

When you took her home at night, you again helped her in and out of the car, kissed her good night and whispered some "sweet somethings" in her ear.

Now that you are married, what do you do for romance? Do you even know what she finds romantic? Do you have a date night? Do you plan it, or do you let her do all the leg work? Do you hire the baby-sitter? Do you shave and shower just for her? Do you give her plenty of time to prepare? Do you take her to romantic places or to the local truck stop?

Do you ever bring her little gifts for no reason, except that you love her? Do you kiss her, and I mean *really* kiss her when you leave for work? You might be interested to know that surveys find men who really kiss their wives before leaving for work live five year longer than men who don't.[3]

You see, the things you did for your sweetie before you were married are the things that wooed her to the altar. Oh, I'm not belittling love, but she fell in love with that wonderfully romantic man who promised to love and cherish her until "death do us part."

Oftentimes, men pursue challenges much like they do a golf game. They always want a bigger and better score, bigger and better golf courses, bigger and better clubs and golf carts. God created a desire in men to be conquerors, and they do just that. A man who has wooed a woman to the altar has "conquered."

While the husband, whose conquering spirit soars at the prospect of each new challenge, is now ready to go on to bigger and better things—his career, ministry or a new business venture—his wife fully expects that wooing, that romancing, to continue. But in the midst of all his other pursuits, he sometimes forgets to continue wooing his sweetie, and now she suddenly isn't so sweet.

She becomes hurt and frustrated and, in her confusion, probably makes all kinds of false accusations to her husband. She blames him for no longer loving her, for ignoring her needs and for loving work, or whatever he's trying to conquer, more than her. To make matters worse, if she is the least bit insecure, her woes will be magnified immensely.

Because she fell in love with the man who wooed her and he fell in love with that sweet little girl who thought the sun rose and set with him, disillusionment sets in. Disappointments and discouragement become the norm. Romance has long since gone out the door, and they both begin to wonder if they are still in love.

Though loving someone doesn't necessarily mean you are "in love" with him or her, being "in love" can continue. But it takes work, and it takes romance to keep the sizzle in the midst of that work.

Since Jesus is your example and He is continually wooing us, His bride, and God commands you to love your wife as Christ loves the church (Eph. 5:25), then guess who had better make romance his top priority?

FIND OUT HER IDEA OF ROMANCE

Stop and consider for a moment what your wife would classify as romantic. I have already mentioned that atmosphere is important in a restaurant, but it is just as important in your actions and especially in your bedroom. For your actions to be romantic, you need to be able to touch her heart, or her emotions—her mind.

A friend of mine told me the sweetest story of how her husband appealed to her romantic mood. He was out of town on business and expecting her to join him on the trip the following week. He knew how much she loved to cross-stitch and that each time she went into a new town she enjoyed getting a cross-stitch pattern depicting some part of that town, usually a tourist attraction.

So he scouted out the stores the week before she arrived. When she got there, he took her to a store that had exactly what she wanted. To her, this was romantic. It ministered to her heart because it took forethought, understanding of what she liked and a special trip to scout out the stores in a town they had never visited before. He could have just waited until she arrived and let her do it while he was working during the day. Instead, he used some ingenuity and, most of all, much love. He met her need, and she knew he was thinking of her even while she wasn't near him.

Later she decided she would like to try something new and romantic on one of their special weekends away together. She bought some fragrant candles for their motel room. When he was already in bed, and the fire in the fireplace had dwindled down to a few embers, she lit one of the candles. Nearly asleep, he smelled the candle and awakened with a start, thinking something was burning. Knowing the fireplace wasn't still going, he quickly said,

"Is something in this room on fire?" Well, that ruined the romance for the night!

So on their next trip, she again took a candle, waited for him to get into bed and lit it. This time they were in a warmer state, and the windows were open. He began sniffing as he lay there in bed and said, "Someone must be barbecuing outside in the neighborhood." Needless to say, she decided candles just weren't going to do it for them.

This couple had one good romantic experience and two that didn't pan out so well.

The candle incidents were something she thought would add a special romantic touch, but for him, who wasn't aware she was lighting them, the candles only triggered different thoughts—certainly not romantic ones.

The point is, what is romantic to one is not necessarily so in the mind of the other.

Even what appeals to one woman may not appeal to another. The woman in this story is my good friend, and we are constantly comparing what appeals to our romantic moods. We are much alike in many ways—in personality and in spiritual desires—but when it comes to romance, we see things so differently. And this is okay because God created each one of us to be unique.

Romance doesn't need to cost a lot of money, just a lot of thought. When Glenn and I were continually traveling and ministering on the road, it was difficult to find romantic times together. One time, however, Glenn found a romantic way to show he was thinking of me. He went out in the woods behind the motel where we were staying and picked a beautiful, big, four-leaf clover. He thought it was so pretty and unusual, so he brought it to me. I kept that clover in my Bible for years. Another time, he brought me some wildflowers that were near our motel.

He might buy me my favorite candy bar or send me a beautiful card or take our clothes to the Laundromat while I stay at the motel and prepare to teach in some church service. It isn't the money spent but the thought that counts. Appealing to the romantic side or to the little girl within her is important.

Buy Her Gifts and Cards

I realize that men who are handy with tools enjoy getting the latest electrical gadget or tool for gifts, but most women don't want "tools" for their anniversaries or Christmas or their birthdays—and certainly not for Valentine's Day. There may be some exceptions, but in general, women want romantic gifts—maybe a stuffed animal, a collector's doll, a piece of jewelry, clothes, perfume or a romantic, sentimental or cute card. Just find out what your wife likes, what appeals to her romantic moods and think of that when you select anything for her.

Take Her out on Weekly Dates

No matter how busy your lives are or how long you've been married, make time to have a weekly date. You can do anything from going to the movies to taking romantic walks. You can go bowling or go out for dinner. You can even make a romantic night of it at home with the fire roaring, just enjoying a romantic video.

Schedule one night every week for dating your sweetheart, and guard that precious time. You may be surprised at how much this simple gesture will revive your wedded bliss.

Cultivate the Four Elements of Romance

One man wrote that there are four elements to romance. They are dating, doing the unexpected, doing the impractical and creativity.[4] These aren't really so hard to put into action.

The dating part takes perseverance to ensure that nothing else tries to steal that time. But as you diligently guard this time, you'll find that others will respect your decision. If you choose to double date or go to a couples' outing on your date night, that should be your choice. Don't allow anyone else to make that choice for you. And make certain you both want to be a part of that event before one of you commits to it.

Doing the unexpected shouldn't be difficult or costly. You could buy her an unexpected gift, send her a little note in the laundry basket, pack her lunch someday before she goes to work, iron her clothes or draw a bubble bath for her and insist she spend thirty minutes in it. If you draw a bath for her, you could even add a fragrant candle to the room and turn out the lights.

Doing the impractical could be buying roses that are usually pretty costly or going on a motel date right in the town where you live. You don't need any clothes, just perhaps a bottle of sparkling cider or white grape juice, two goblets and a bucket of ice. Or how about a Jacuzzi date at a place where you can rent the room and have it all to yourself? What about a date up on the highest point in (or out of) town, just having fun in the car?

What about sending the kids off to a grandparent's or neighbor's house and lighting the fire, setting the table with your finest china, sending out for a catered meal, turning on your favorite dance music and waltzing your sweetie around? If she isn't overly modest and she is a good dancer, what about buying her a sexy negligee and asking her to dance for you, accompanied by some alluring music?

Creativity will depend on your thoughtfulness and understanding her needs. Some handpicked flowers from your own backyard in a pretty vase can be a piece of art to your wife's eyes. What about making an appointment for her to have one of those wonderful facial makeovers? Or what about taking her to one of those shops where they take great photographs after they have fixed someone up?

Another creative thing that would appeal to some women is simply putting together a scrapbook of your wife's life, using pictures from her childhood on up. Or you could write a wonderful letter about how much you appreciate her and list your reasons—her good qualities, how proud you feel when you are out with her. If you are handy with woodworking, something you make especially for her would be a beautiful memento.

One man I heard about planned a weekend away with his wife, arranged for the kids' care, packed her suitcase, hid everything from her and suddenly showed up at her job early on Friday afternoon and announced to her that they were leaving town. They went to some romantic spot and had a marvelous time. Yes, it took money; but more than that, it took creativity.

A Story of Romance

Two very special friends of Glenn's and mine, with hearts of the most faithful, true and pure servants, have recently experienced real romance blooming in their marriage. We have known them for years. Their children are now married and are on their own, yet the couple's love for one other is growing beautifully.

Years ago, as the coordinators of the helps ministry in the church Glenn and I pastored, they took charge of everything, making our jobs very easy. We are eternally grateful to them for all they did to help us.

Later, however, they took over and successfully pastored two churches that were having difficulties. As a result, this couple had some financial difficulties.

Nevertheless, the husband decided that he wanted to surprise his wife for their twenty-fifth anniversary with a cruise to Nassau. Because they had encountered some financial difficulties and were just overcoming them, the feat looked impossible, but the husband is a man of faith who knew that all things were possible through God and that faith works through love. His love for his wife was great and he wanted to do something very special for her. So he began secretly putting money away for the cruise. He even worked a second job in the evenings in addition to his full-time job. His wife never suspected what he was doing and thought the second job was just to catch up on the bills.

A few weeks before they were scheduled to leave he told her that after a year of saving he wanted to buy her some new clothes because they were going on the cruise of their dreams. To say the least, his wife was really surprised and thrilled at this romantic display of her husband's love.

Their story touched my heart because it was so sweet and so romantic. All of the elements of romance—surprise, the impractical, dating and creativity—came into play here. It was an unexpected surprise to his wife. It was impractical, especially for a couple who had struggled over the years with their finances. This cruise was certainly going to be one long date for them, culminating years of dedication and perseverance in adverse situations. Creativity abounded in the manner in which the husband saved by working a second job, planned every detail and made sure he had plenty of money for his wife to buy a new wardrobe of clothes.

Today they are one happy couple because romance has been rekindled, and a new spark has set their hearts aflame. What a joy it is to see two dear servants of God enjoying the fruit of their labor of love in such a romantic way. God is truly a rewarder of those who diligently seek Him. (Heb. 11:6.)

HELP HER GET IN THE MOOD

Another thing you can do, which may take a little creativity, is to try to see your bedroom as your wife sees it. Earlier I mentioned that bedroom atmosphere is important for women. For a woman who works inside of her home and possibly outside, she needs a little change of scenery when she walks into her bedroom, so allow her to decorate the bedroom to suit her romantic needs or her personality. If it is frillier than you like it, it will be worth it when she joins you in bed. She may feel down when she finishes her household tasks, but walking into a romantic bedroom filled with flowers, candles and satin could suddenly lift her spirits and turn her mind to other things.

THE DOS AND DON'TS OF ROMANCE

Besides a romantic setting, the following are some other helpful hints about what you can do, and what you shouldn't do to try to interest your sweetheart in sexual activity.

1. Don't ignore her needs all day and expect a good night in bed that evening.

2. Do encourage her as a woman, a wife and a mother whenever you can.

3. Don't comment on her being overweight. If she is, it will only frustrate her and cause resentment. She already knows she is overweight.

   I know a woman who is very overweight, but who told me that when her husband makes love to her she feels thin and beautiful. Now that is quite a compliment for that man. Even though I think this particular woman is pretty, she doesn't feel that way because of her weight problem, but his lovemaking makes her feel that way regardless.

4. Do remember to keep your body clean, use cologne, shave, and keep your nails clipped short and smooth and your hands softened with lotion. Rough hands or long nails can irritate the intimate places on a woman's body.

5. Don't massage your wife with roughness, but remember to caress her lightly.

6. Do start romancing her early in the day, not at 10:30 P.M.

7. Don't allow rudeness, belching loudly, poor table manners, unkind remarks or gestures to be a part

of your routine. If it happens, at least have the grace to excuse yourself.

8. Do create within her an image of her being a romantic lover. Call her some pet name, buy her a pretty gown or find some creative way to improve her image of herself as a lover.
9. Don't place your full weight on her during intercourse. You are heavier than you think, and it can be uncomfortable enough to extinguish her "flame."
10. Do hug and kiss her at times other than when you desire sex.
11. Don't attempt internal vaginal stimulation prematurely.
12. Do try to keep your body in somewhat good shape. A nude pot belly may turn a woman off. The Shulamite commented on Solomon's belly being like ivory, and to be like ivory means to be flat and firm, not just white.[5]
13. Don't demand she do things to you in bed that she disagrees with or feels uncomfortable doing.
14. Do give her an evening or a Saturday off while you watch the kids, make dinner and put the kids to bed.
15. Don't leave your clothes all over, as you did when you were a kid, and expect her to pick up after you, as your mother did.

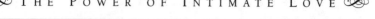

16. Do be willing to try new sexual positions.

17. Don't allow her to second guess your every move when you are involved in foreplay. Keep her guessing as you tease her with your caresses.

18. Do telephone her from work and call her some passionate name or tell her how special she is to you.

19. Don't allow your mind to wander during foreplay or intercourse. Keep your mind and your heart on what you are doing.

20. Do allow your love to caress her, whether you are using your lips, your hands or your genitals. She needs to feel the penetration of your love just as much as the penetration of your penis.

By following these guidelines, you will not only bring all of the elements of romance into the marriage bed, but you will bring the God-kind of love as well.

CHAPTER 6

Exploring Acceptable Sexual Behavior

> **Marriage is honourable in all, and the bed undefiled: but whoremongers and adulterers God will judge.**
>
> **Hebrews 13:4**

Glenn and I have taught marriage seminars for thousands of people and spoken with hundreds afterwards, and we have counseled married couples and singles. Consistently, we are asked, in one way or another, "What is acceptable sexual behavior?" Specifically, we are frequently asked what we think about oral sex, but what we think is not the issue. What *God* has to say about it in His Word is what matters.

WHAT DOES GOD'S WORD SAY?

Verse 4 of Hebrews 13 is most often quoted regarding the topic of oral sex.

Marriage is honourable in all, and the bed undefiled: but whoremongers and adulterers God will judge.

Some preach that this verse means "anything goes" in the marriage bed. Others say it means the marriage bed is defiled or dishonored if certain things are done, and they usually define those "certain things" as oral sex.

I have actually heard some ministers admit that while oral sex isn't actually referred to here, that doesn't mean it is all right. They proceed to say that the mouth was meant for praising God, not for sex. I often wondered how they managed to eat their meals if that is the only thing the mouth was created for. And does this philosophy mean that we must stop kissing? It's hard to praise God and kiss your mate with your mouth at the same time.

Some define oral sex differently than others. Some would include kissing of any place other than the lips as oral sex, while others consider kissing of the genital area to be oral sex. For the sake of clarity, I will use Clifford and Joyce Penner's definition from their book *The Gift of Sex:*

"Oral sex or oral stimulation of your partner's genitals with your mouth, lips, and tongue. The man may stimulate the woman's clitoris and the opening of the vagina with his tongue, or the woman may pleasure the man's penis with her mouth."[1]

As Glenn studied the Word concerning God's directives regarding this controversial topic, he found Hebrews 13:4 to actually be a summation of God's viewpoint of what is allowed in marital sex. His studies revealed the following version, which he refers to as the Glenn Brown paraphrase:

> Marriage is the honorable way to keep your sexual intercourse pure. God will judge all those that have sexual intercourse outside of the marital relationship.

In a nutshell, the above verse, which is as accurate to the Greek as possible, gives the entire counsel of God on the subject. Other verses allude to other aspects, which we will look into, but as a whole, this verse sums it up.

WHAT ABOUT ORAL SEX IN HOMOSEXUALITY?

Other verses definitely warn against incest, bestiality, fornication, adultery and homosexuality. For the sake of brevity, we will only look at homosexuality here. Romans 1:21-27 states,

> **Because that, when they knew God, they glorified him not as God, neither were thankful; but became vain in their imaginations, and their foolish heart was darkened. Professing themselves to be wise, they became fools, and changed the glory of the incorruptible God into an image made like to corruptible man, and to birds, and four-footed beasts, and creeping things. Wherefore God also gave them up unto uncleanness through the lusts of their own hearts, to dishonour their own bodies between themselves: who changed the truth of God into a lie, and worshipped and served**

> **the creature more than the Creator, who is blessed for ever. Amen.**
>
> **For this cause God gave them up unto vile affections: for even their women did change the natural use into that which is against nature: and likewise also the men, leaving the natural use of the woman, burned in their lust one toward another; men with men working that which is unseemly, and receiving in themselves that recompence of their error which was meet.**

Most teachers who preach against oral sex use these verses to support their position, but a close look reveals that God is speaking against the misuse of intercourse. He clearly shows it is *whom* one has sex with that leads to sin. Men with men or women with women is "changing the natural use" and going against what God originally intended. Lustful spirits are also involved; hence, the terminology, "burned in their lust one toward another." The word *burned* literally means "burned out." The term is used in a way which is terrible in its intensity and the preposition *out* attached to the verb *burn* in the Greek indicates the rage of the lust.[2]

The word *lust* here means "reaching out after something with the purpose of appropriating it for oneself."[3] This was the primary motive behind the sex taking place. Husbands and wives are not to lust after each other, but to love one another as God has ordained. Love, not lust, is God's way. Anything other than what He has ordained is sin, and there are consequences to sin.

Romans 1:26-27 shows us that the consequence of persisting to misuse sex is that God finally "gave them up unto vile affections," or their "passions of dishonor." They weren't merely given over to the *vile affections*, but also to the diseased condition out of which the lusts sprang.[4]

Lesbians and homosexuals lust after one another and do that which the Bible calls *unseemly*. Interestingly enough the word *unseemly* means "want of form" or "disfigurement."[5] God formed the male and female bodies to fit together in perfect form. Intercourse brings them together into one flesh, one figure, the way God intended. There is not disfigurement in marital sex as there is in homosexuality and lesbianism.

The only way that a woman can be together with another woman is through the use of manual stimulation and oral sex. Men lusting after men results in manual stimulation, oral sex and sometimes anal sex. Such behavior is unseemly and offensive to God, who created *men and women* to be one form, one flesh, not women with women or men with men.

What About Oral Sex in Foreplay?

So we know that God does not permit homosexuality, but how do we know what He intended for husbands and wives to enjoy and what He restricted in their sexual activities. The first thing to consider is this: If He had certain guidelines for marital physical intimacy, wouldn't

He have clearly stated them for us? He definitely wrote certain things which are sin in His eyes so we would know we aren't to partake in them, yet He appears to be relatively silent on the subject of oral sex even though there are certain verses which could be interpreted to relate to oral sex. We will look at those later in this chapter.

The second thing to consider is what does "one flesh" literally mean? How can a man and woman be one flesh? The answer to this question is fairly obvious. God intended man to penetrate woman by inserting his penis into her vagina to become "one flesh." This act is sexual intercourse.

But foreplay is a different matter, and this is where there are no evident restrictions in the Word. However, we come into marriage with certain preconceived notions, and—depending on our previous sexual experiences, backgrounds and circumstances—our moral standards could vary vastly.

One person's convictions or feelings about sex can't be forced on another, especially in the marriage bed. Our standard should always be the Word of God, but what one person can freely do in faith another might not feel is right for him or her.

FOLLOW THE LAW OF LOVE

This is where the law of love enter the picture. Romans 14:12-14 states:

> **So then every one of us shall give account of himself to God. Let us not therefore judge one another any more: but judge this rather, that no man put a stumblingblock or an occasion to fall in his brother's way. I know, and am persuaded by the Lord Jesus, that there is nothing unclean of itself: but to him that esteemeth any thing to be unclean, to him it is unclean.**

Verse 22 states:

> **Hast thou faith? have it to thyself before God. Happy is he that condemneth not himself in that thing which he alloweth.**

The context of this text is about food, but the principle is the same for any area of your life. Your convictions must never be forced on one another, nor can you allow another to force his or hers on you. You must follow after peace (v. 19) and the things which bring peace in your marriage, but never violate your own will and convictions. That is why verse 23 states, **Whatsoever is not of faith is sin.** So if you can't do something in faith before God, then to you it is sin. First Corinthians 10:28-29 emphasizes the same truth: We can't use our liberty to judge another man's conscience. Verse 31 states, **Whatsoever ye do, do all to the glory of God.**

Unfortunately, some people have yet to understand that sexual intercourse, created by God himself, brings glory to God. Their own inhibitions prevent them from enjoying freedom in bed with their mates, so even most foreplay is restricted for them. But God created our bodies to be enjoyed by one another in the marriage relationship. He created us for intimacy and openness with one another.

Adam and Eve were naked and not ashamed before one another. (Gen. 2:25.) Some feel this verse implies they were covered with the glory of God, so they weren't really naked. Others feel it means they were open in every area toward one another and that they had nothing to hide.

When sin entered the world, sexual perversion was close behind. But intercourse is not perverted when it's between husband and wife. God wants us to be free with one another in the sexual area as with all areas of our marriage.

Most people who ask us about oral sex usually want to force their mates to do something to them against the other's will. This is not love, but it could be lust. Love gives, then receives. Lust takes, regardless of the other's feelings.

For some, oral sex has evil connotations. For some it is an unpleasant reminder of past sexual promiscuity, and for some it is simply uncomfortable or embarrassing. Others freely enjoy it without any sense of guilt. They utilize it in foreplay to express their passion and tender love toward each other with joy and freedom.

ORAL SEX IN THE SONG OF SOLOMON

Some scholars feel Solomon and the Shulamite enjoyed oral sex in foreplay. In the Song of Solomon 4:5,

Solomon says to the Shulamite, **Thy two breasts are like two young roes that are twins, which feed among the lilies.** *Roes* here means fawns or young gazelles. This specific reference was to the dorcas gazelle, a graceful, beautiful animal considered a delicacy served at Solomon's table. These creatures have a frolicking behavior that makes them irresistible to the beholder and attracts him to come near and touch them.[6]

According to Joseph Dillow in his book *Solomon on Sex:*

> Casual reflections on the many associations connected with the words *gazelle* and *lilies* make his description of his wife's breasts pregnant with beautiful connotations. They are very curvaceous like the lily. Their beauty creates within his heart a desire to reach out and fondle them as one would a gazelle feeding by a brook. The notion of frolicksomeness suggests sexual playfulness. The fact that gazelles were served as a delicacy at Solomon's table suggests his desire to caress them with his lips and tongue. As gazelles were warm and affectionate, so was the Shulamite as a sexual partner.[7]

Most women find a man's caressing and kissing their breasts to be stimulating and enjoyable. However, if one member of a marriage dislikes oral sex, it is usually the woman, not the man. In foreplay, women often draw the line at oral genital stimulation. It appears that the Shulamite did not have this reservation.

Again, quoting from Joseph Dillow's book:

> The female genitals are referred to in 5:1 as a "garden" and in 4:13 as "shoots." In both passages, myrrh and frankincense are described as characteristic scents of her "garden."[8]

In the Song of Solomon 4:12, Solomon says, **A garden inclosed is my sister, my spouse...** He refers to the fact that she is a virgin since her garden is her vagina, which he continues to describe in the same verse as **a spring shut up, a fountain sealed.**

To the Hebrew mind, gardens were considered beautiful. In describing the Shulamite's vagina as a garden, Solomon is saying that it is beautiful, just like the flowered gardens of the East. He also views it as a source of refreshment for him to experience, because gardens were often shaded, restful places that refreshed one's body and mind. Carefully cultivated Eastern gardens yielded wonderfully delicious fruits, and he desires the Shulamite's garden of delicious "fruits," or sexual pleasures, when cultivated.

For Solomon, making love with the Shulamite was much like entering a paradise where secret pleasures abounded. They were hidden from everyone but Solomon, the new owner of the fruitful garden. As we noted in chapter 1, Solomon referred to his bride's garden as an orchard of pomegranates, a delicious fruit. This is a delicate reference to oral sex, or the stimulation of the genitals with the mouth, lips and tongue.[9]

Clifford and Joyce Penner, authors of *The Gift of Sex,* state in their book:

> Solomon in the Song of Solomon refers continually to enjoying the delights of his lover's body. He speaks of feeding among the lilies (4:5). His partner says, "Awake, north wind, and come, south wind. Blow on my garden, that its fragrance may spread abroad. Let my lover come into his garden and taste its choice fruits" (4:16). In the following verse King Solomon says, "I have come into my garden.... I gather my myrrh with my spices. I have eaten my honeycomb and my honey; I have drunk my wine and my milk" (5:1). His lover responds, "Eat, O friends, and drink; drink your fill, O lovers." Many references speak of the oral delights of one's lover, and the enjoyment of her full body. Every part is talked about: hair, lips, neck, breasts, stomach, legs, feet. The lovers usually refer to the genitals as the "garden of spices." The book speaks of total body involvement. For some of us this freedom seems strange, unusual, and not part of the natural order.

The Scriptures are not clear on the matter of oral sex, and so it is one of those gray areas where various biblical teachings will come into play. The principle of what is loving and caring for the other person must be addressed. On the other hand, the teaching that our bodies are each other's to enjoy must also be incorporated.

The Penners write:

> One thing we would caution against. Many people use Christian or moral argument to defend against an activity which is personally troublesome

> to them. Often their moral arguments, though relatively weak, keep them from dealing with the *real issues* of emotional conflict. By finding some obscure passage or unique interpretation, they avoid working through their own personal reason for the position they hold. While it is sometimes easier to call on an outside authority, this can cause a person to avoid facing the genuine issues that are present and need to be discussed with one's spouse.[11]

The Penners are Spirit-filled, Christian sex therapists who conduct marriage enrichment seminars and help people deal with trouble areas by giving detailed instructions on how to deal with them. He is a clinical psychologist and consultant, and she has a master's degree in nursing. I highly recommend their entire book, which has detailed information about how our bodies function sexually in addition to good basic teaching on the spiritual and emotional arenas of sexual intimacy.

The important thing to remember here is that oral sex should be discussed in the light of foreplay and not the final act of physical intimacy. Equally important is the fact that oral sex isn't a necessary part of foreplay, nor should it be considered essential to intercourse. I believe, however, that it can be an option for those couples who *both* desire it.

Oral Sex and Cleanliness

Some questions that often arise about oral sex are regarding cleanliness. According to the Penners,

> There are three types of systems in the genital area: sterile, clean and contaminated. The urinary system is sterile; that is, it has no microorganisms. The reproductive system, which includes the penis or the vagina, is clean. It is free of any disease-producing microorganisms. Finally, the rectal area and the mouth are contaminated with disease-producing microorganisms. Therefore, if the body is cleanly washed and there are no infections present, contamination of the mouth from the genitals is impossible. If contamination takes place because of infection, it will usually be communicated from the mouth to the genitals rather than from the genitals to the mouth.[12]

GET IN AGREEMENT WITH YOUR MATE

I've included this discussion on oral sex because of the many questions we hear regarding the subject. It isn't intended to persuade anyone one way or the other or to persuade anyone's mate in any way. If an otherwise happily married couple cannot reach an agreement on this issue, the first thing they should do is pray together. If they still can't agree or they don't feel they have enough answers or assurance from God regarding their stand, they should make an appointment with their pastor or a good Christian counselor. So many issues are far more important than this one, yet so many marriages seem to be plagued with disagreement regarding it.

Our marriage relationships and mutually satisfying levels of sexual intimacy are more important than individual preferences regarding oral sex. Pursuing the issue or insisting on our own way only increases the pressure on our mates. It simply isn't worth risking our marriages over something that is simply not essential to sexual fulfillment.

Freedom means different things to different people. God wants us to be free in our lovemaking and to enjoy each other's bodies as much as possible. Jesus came to set us free from fear, condemnation, guilt and sin. He came to give us abundance of life, and that abundant life should be included in our sexual intimacy.

It seems clear to me that in this gray area, God has left the decision up to us. Keeping in mind the hindrances discussed earlier in this chapter, we might not all decide alike; but God, who created us so differently, understands our needs, our ethnic backgrounds, our racial differences, our moral preferences, our comfort zones and our own particular feelings about the entire issue.

God cares for us intensely. He desires His best for marriages. His best should motivate us in the marriage bed, just as it should in other areas of our lives. His love never fails, and if we apply it to our sexual relationships, we will never fail. We must not allow this to be a stumbling block to our love life and the way we can best express our love for our mate. Love never ever fails.

CHAPTER 7

Bedroom Boredom or Abundant Arousal?

> **Many waters cannot quench love, neither can the floods drown it....**
>
> **Song of Solomon 8:7**

Romance puts a zing into marriage. It keeps that flame burning when the embers are about to die out. It adds a spark to the engines when they are feeling cold and sluggish. But the actions that most people identify as romantic aren't necessary for a good marriage if there is sufficient love, mutual respect, trust, commitment and understanding.

TRUE ROMANCE IS MUCH MORE THAN ACTIONS

As a matter of fact, true romance is so much more than anything we can do. In a discussion with a friend about true romance, she related that when she first married she wanted her husband to be very romantic, but he just never did really seem to be that way. She continued by saying that even though he wasn't romantic, he was very tender and sentimental and was a great husband.

Her way of adapting to the lack of obvious romance in their marriage was looking at her husband's good points and embracing these. She was full of praise for his thoughtfulness toward her, and even though he didn't often tell her he loved her, she never doubted his love. He did at times do things for her that she considered romantic, but she believes that the things one does that are considered romantic don't always assure one of a good marriage.

This friend pointed out that she knew of someone who was always hugging and kissing his mate and that she once was very jealous of this because he did it in front of others. But today this same couple is divorced. She concluded that the affection displayed openly didn't go very deep on the inside.

True romance is much more than actions. If the heart isn't in it, it won't work. If a wife demands romance from her husband and he reciprocates just to get her off his back, or vice versa, then it really isn't true romance. *True romance comes from the heart.*

I think my friend's solution to her husband's lack of romance is a good one. Marriage is about mutual, intimate love, about sharing with each other—spirit, soul and body—and, most of all, about commitment and trust.

Concentrate on Your Blessings

Let's face it, women, the majority of men aren't as romantic as most women. I realize there are exceptions, but I'm speaking in general. And some men may never come up with any romantic notions even after they have read a book on it. So this is where my friend's great attitude comes in. She felt she was very much compensated because of her husband's other good qualities. She chose to concentrate on those qualities rather than his lack of romance.

Obviously she'd made that choice years before, because they'd been married a long time and had a great marriage. But what if she hadn't chosen to overlook the lack of romance and actually focused only on that? What if she had decided to look elsewhere for romance? What if she had become so absorbed in romance novels that she'd felt continually unhappy and deprived?

I have observed some women who are bored with their husbands, who don't want to make love with them and who complain about the lack of romance in their relationship. These women are headed for trouble if they continue going in the same direction.

If this describes you, I strongly advise you to begin to assess your husband's best traits and concentrate on them. Is he faithful to you? Does he provide for you to the best of his ability? Is he a good father? Does he love you? Does he respect you as a woman and treat you well? Is he energetic? Is he fun? Is he understanding, sentimental, kind or generous?

The devil loves it when he can get us to concentrate on lack rather than our blessings. Nothing destroys his power more in our lives than praise and appreciation to God for what we do have. Be thankful to God for the man He has given you. He is a gift from God, and God only gives good gifts. Oh, your husband isn't perfect, but if he is good, thank God for him. Since you aren't perfect, that sort of keeps things even, doesn't it?

SUGGESTIONS FOR THE INCURABLE ROMANTIC

Since opposites usually attract, it is unlikely that both parties are incurably romantic. However, just because your mate isn't romantic doesn't mean you can't bring some romance into your relationship.

First, since men's and women's ideas of romance often differ, find out what pleases your mate. For instance, as a woman, a candlelight dinner usually seems romantic. Suppose you cook a lavish meal, set your finest tableware out and light some candles. Let's say you have also put on a nice outfit, and you are ready for a truly romantic evening with your husband.

In he walks and the first thing out of his mouth is "What's the occasion?" Maybe it is even something more like "What is it you want from me?" or "Is something wrong?" It would be easy for a romantic woman, full of expectations, to get upset or be disappointed at this point in the evening, but you have to consider several things.

First of all, if he isn't romantic according to you, then your idea of romance isn't his idea. When it comes to dinner, most men aren't concerned about atmosphere. They just want good food.

So a wise woman might give the unromantic husband a hint, or warning, that she is planning a special meal for the two of them that night. A wise woman might also do something that really appeals to him—rub his back, kiss him soundly, perhaps kiss his neck and ears while she is at it, smile brightly and compliment him on his good looks–and then ask about his day with *real* interest.

Maybe a wise woman would suggest a shower together to refresh them before dinner. Maybe she would slip into something alluring. Maybe she would play his favorite music, cook his favorite dish (even if it doesn't seem like a romantic meal), fix her hair just the way he likes it, offer to watch Monday night TV with him or join him in whatever he likes to do.

DON'T IGNORE HIM—JOIN HIM

There are plenty of things a woman can do to just *be* with her husband. I know one woman who feels very romantic toward her husband when they are outside working in the yard together. She was raised on a farm, so her man's display of physical strength appeals to her. I imagine some men would do a lot more yard work if they knew the potential was there to light a fire in their wives.

Sometimes men aren't too interested in paying a lot of attention to their wives because their wives seem to ignore them. In fact, many husbands feel pretty neglected much of the time. The kids seem to get all of the attention. Does this shoe fit your marriage? If so, find some way to give him the attention he needs and deserves from you—outside and inside of the bedroom.

What About Your Husband's Fantasies?

Are you and your beloved experiencing abundant arousal or bedroom boredom? Sometimes bedroom boredom has nothing to do with romance. Sometimes it is simply because one person or the other or maybe both are in a rut. If your sex life is always the same and, in fact, you can predict exactly what will happen next, you are definitely in a rut, and things could get boring.

Have you ever considered what your mate's personal fantasies are? Now, please don't think I'm talking about kinky sex or whips, chains and handcuffs. No, I don't personally feel a Christian marriage has need of those in bed or in any aspect of a couple's sex life.

While we are on the subject, I want to address the question of using vibrators to enhance lovemaking. Again, the Word of God has no specifics on the subject, but I personally see no need for them when we have hands, lips and other great body parts to successfully heighten our intimate sexual encounters. I have never personally used a vibrator, but it seems to me they would take away some of the fun of natural stimulation.

Sexual fantasies don't have to be evil or painful. Suppose a man would just love to see his wife dancing for him in a flimsy gown, but he has never had the nerve to ask her because he fears she would reject the whole idea. Is there anything wrong with a wife dancing in the privacy of her bedroom before her husband?

Before some of you women get puritanical on me, please read the Song of Solomon 6:13 NIV. The Shulamite is saying, **Why would you gaze on the Shulammite as on the dance of the Mahanaim?** In *Solomon on Sex,* Joseph Dillow states that the Shulamite and Solomon are alone and that she "desires to make love with her husband and aggressively takes the initiative. As part of their love play, and as her way of arousing her husband's sexual interest, she dances before him."[1]

Dillow then goes on to explain that the phrase *two companies* is a Hebrew word *mahanaim,* which was a town from which David fled as a fugitive from Absalom as mentioned in 2 Samuel 17:24. He also mentions that joy and dancing were inseparable in the Old Testament or Eastern mind-set. Joy, in this sense, was a holy joy in a spiritual sense as well as a happy feeling.[2]

Reading further in Song of Solomon 6, you will see how Solomon responds to his wife's dancing before him. He begins to comment on the beauty of her feet, the curves of her hips, the work of her hands, navel, hair, head, nose, eyes, neck, breasts, belly and thighs. He really doesn't leave out much. It seems he certainly enjoyed this sexual love play. He probably especially loved the idea of her aggressive initiation toward him sexually. I'm sure few men would complain about their wives' dancing before them in this manner.

Perhaps your husband's fantasy is to see you model some jewelry in the nude. Maybe he'd just like to see you in a coat with nothing on underneath.

Maybe just once he would like to make love with the lights on, which many women find very unromantic. Or suppose he prefers sex in the morning or afternoon rather than at night? I heard Pat Harrison say one time, "Why not be an afternoon delight, ladies, rather than a nightly dread?"

Now, most women never think of things like that to satisfy their husband's fantasies. Wives, it will do your marriage good to find out your husband's specific fantasy and help make his dream come true. The experience might just be a dream-come-true for you too.

WHAT ABOUT YOUR WIFE'S FANTASIES?

Now husbands, what are your wife's fantasies? Would she like you to put on silk shorts? Maybe she would like you to dance before her. What about the two of you dancing in your bedroom accompanied by some mood music? There are some really good romantic love songs out by Christian recording artists. Maybe she would like you to slowly remove her clothes. Maybe she'd like to experiment with some of those flavorful lotions or whipped cream.

Perhaps none of these things excites you, but have you asked your mate what he or she thinks about it?

What about reading the Song of Solomon together and inserting your own words or expressions to describe your mate's body parts. Now, be kind and encouraging. This could prove to be a fun time and could lead to some real insights about each other. You may just find out what your mate really loves about you and your body but never expressed quite that way before. Giving and receiving such approval will be sure to create within both of you a deeper sense of security, which will lead to a more satisfying sexual relationship.

DON'T LET THE SUN GO DOWN ON YOUR ANGER

However, if sex isn't presently satisfying for you, this dissatisfaction undoubtedly carries over into all areas of your married life. Sometimes resentment can try to creep in over sexual dissatisfaction or other disagreements. Even if the differences are not sexual, they will still affect your sexual enjoyment.

Bitterness, anger, rejection, resentments, mistrust and unforgiveness will all affect sexual relationships. Paul, in his letter to the Ephesians, admonishes us to sin not though we be angry, and not to let the sun go down upon our anger. (Eph. 4:26.) In other words, Paul was saying we should deal with our anger through constructive communication and resolve issues before each day is over.

It is especially important to resolve differences before you engage in sexual activity with your spouse. Whether consciously or unconsciously, if you are harboring unforgiveness and any other ill feelings toward your mate, you will display them during intercourse and your mate will sense them. Your tenderness and consideration will be absent. Your desire to please each other will be replaced by selfish desire. Anger will be displayed in rough treatment or hurried sex. Resentment will be expressed as either boredom or apathy—a lack of interest or involvement.

I believe such expression of the feelings described above are a misuse of sexual intimacy. I don't believe God takes this lightly. He has shown us that sexual intercourse between husbands and wives is a holy act that should always be accompanied by love at the highest level. Love forgives fully and restores one to right standing, just as the Author of perfect love does.

Doing things God's way always works. And love always works. It never fails. I can't imagine anything more wonderful, fulfilling and satisfying to us than when Jesus, our Bridegroom, returns for us, His bride. As we come together for the wedding feast, the ecstasy will be incomparable to anything we have experienced in the natural world. Can you even imagine being bored, disinterested or upset with our wonderful Groom? It would be unthinkable for us to remain in unforgiveness, resentment, bitterness, anger or disinterest in this most intimate time.

Since God has compared Jesus to the husband and the bride of Christ to the wife, do we dare hold onto those feelings that would hinder ecstasy with our mates here on earth? Do we have the right to allow those things to take away what He has created to be holy, pure and good? Do we dare allow intimate times to become stale and regard them as unimportant, something to be rushed or added to our day just because our mates insist on having their own way? Can selfishness have any part in something which God calls holy?

Take Responsibility for Your Attitude

Boredom is a state of mind, not necessarily a summation of the true situation. Boredom usually comes from our own restlessness or unfulfilled needs and appetites. Monotonous actions often stem from a lack of knowledge and/or experience or from a lack of creativity. But God, the Creator of all, has put His creativity within us and given us His Word and His Holy Spirit to teach us what we need to know to be good lovers.

His love for us is our example. His wooing of us teaches us the way to true romance. His Spirit within us guides and directs us specifically according to our mate's needs and desires.

If bedroom boredom exists, it is our fault, not God's. If we want that boredom replaced with excitement, beauty and fulfillment, then it is up to us to seek God's help. Don't wait for your mate to initiate change, and don't blame him or her either. Start now by acknowledging your responsibility, and do whatever it takes to turn bedroom boredom around to abundant arousal.

CHAPTER 8

The Power of Sex

> **The wife hath not power of her own body, but the husband: and likewise also the husband hath not power of his own body, but the wife.**
>
> **1 Corinthians 7:4**

Sex is a powerful tool to be used, not abused, in marriage. God created this powerful tool for our pleasure, but just as with any power tool, following instructions is essential. When misuse of a power tool occurs, whether through lack of knowledge or carelessness, that tool can become a dangerous object that can maim or even kill. The misuse of sexual intimacy can be equally destructive to the health of a marriage.

According to modern Jewish writer, Robert Gordis, author of *Love and Sex,* "The role of sex in stimulating men to furthering human progress is mirrored in another Rabbinic epithet, 'the leaven in the dough'...leaven is a source of growth or it can bring decay."[1]

If you are presently married, reflect on your sex life for a while and then ask yourself, *Do my attitudes and actions involving this most intimate part of marriage bring growth or decay?* Ask God to show you any problem areas, even blind spots, that you might not readily recognize. Most of us, both men and women, are guilty of misuse in the sexual area at one time or another.

THE WAYS WIVES MISUSE SEX

Just what does this misuse of sex look like? Well, let's start with the wives. We have already mentioned that having a headache, being too tired or just not being in the mood are some of the excuses wives use, but what about the deeper issues behind those excuses?

Wives, are you withholding sexual intimacy from your husband because you are punishing him for something he did or didn't do? Or are you using sex as a means of manipulating him into giving you something you really want?

In the pages following, I've listed these and other ways wives sometimes misuse sex. Wives, if you identify with any of these examples, it is time to turn things around and begin to use the power tool of sexual intimacy to build up, rather than tear down, your husband and your marriage.

By Withholding Sex To Punish

In 1 Corinthians 7:4, when referring to the fact that husbands and wives have power over one another's bodies, that word *power* actually means "exercise authority upon."[2] But any way one looks at it, the meaning is clear: We belong to our mates.

The Bible never states that we have *dominion* over other human beings. It does say we have dominion over animals in Genesis 1:28. That word actually means "to tread, to tread down; to have dominion, to rule, to bear rule."[3] Dominating is different than exercising authority.

In Luke 10:19 and Mark 16:17-18, Jesus gave us power, or authority, to be used to minister good and to eradicate evil. Paul said we don't war against people, **but against principalities, against powers, against the rulers of the darkness of this world, against wickedness in high places** (Eph. 6:12).

The principles of authority and power, which are found throughout the entire Bible, never give us the right to exercise our wills or take dominion over other human beings. Therefore, when husbands and wives are told they have power over each other's bodies, they must consider exactly what this means. In chapter 6 I discussed the need to operate in the law of love. We aren't to deny one another of sexual intimacy because this places temptation on one another.

The Jewish Code of Law states a protective law for the wife's rights. This code makes for interesting reading and reveals how specifically the ancient rabbis' writings were regarding this most important aspect of marriage.

This particular Jewish Code of Law expounds on Exodus 21:10—**If he take him another wife; her food, her raiment, and her duty of marriage, shall he not diminish**—saying:

> Men of a strong constitution who enjoy the pleasures of life, having profitable pursuits at home and are tax exempt, should perform their marital duty nightly. Laborers who work in the town where they reside, should perform their marital duty twice weekly; but if they are employed in another town, only once a week. Merchants who travel into villages with their mules, to buy grain to be sold in town, and others like them, should perform their marital duty once a week. Men who convey freight on camels from distant places should attend to their marital duty once in thirty days. One must fulfill his marital duty even when his wife is pregnant or nursing. One must not deprive his wife of her conjugal rights, unless she consents to it, and when he has already fulfilled the obligation of propagation. If he deprives his wife thereof, in order to afflict her, he violates the Divine Command.[4]

Apparently, there were some abuses even then, or that last sentence wouldn't have been written.

That first sentence said that wealthy men "should perform their marital duty nightly." Since a prosperous man usually has many decisions to make during the day regarding his businesses, it is easy to see why tensions could easily mount and why he would need the release more often than someone who is using his body in his work.

On the other end of the spectrum, men who performed more menial tasks in their work were to "attend to their marital duty once in thirty days." These men's jobs required them to be out of town, and accommodating for marital intimacy could be a problem because commuting wasn't quite as quick and easy in those days.

Through this law, the rabbis were addressing some of the very real issues and needs of their days, but the basis of that law was the wives' rights. And since the men often had more than one wife, or perhaps concubines, the rabbis were specifically addressing the fact that her needs came first. In essence, then, the ancient writers addressed the needs of both the husband and the wife.

The Old Testament also addressed a woman's menstrual cycle and gave specific instructions for a two-week period of abstinence because she was considered "unclean." So obviously, when the Jewish law stated that the prosperous man was to partake of sex with his wife every night, it was excluding those two weeks.

Today, however, the Scripture in 1 Corinthians 7:5 makes it very clear that the old law of uncleanness does not apply to Christian marriages: **Defraud ye not one the other, except it be with consent for a time, that ye may give yourselves to fasting and prayer; and come together again, that Satan tempt you not for your incontinency.** Paul said the only reason for withholding sexual pleasures was for prayer, and then only by mutual consent.

This Scripture should not be construed to mean that no matter how you treat your spouse, he or she must consent to sexual intimacy with you. On the contrary, sexual intimacy should be based on the law of love, not on selfish desires, and it should flow out of a natural desire created by an atmosphere of love and respect.

I once heard a story of a woman who had waited for her husband to open her car door, which was his custom, but this particular time he didn't. He just looked at her and said loudly, "Well, you can just stay in there until you burn up in this heat, and I still won't open it." Several bystanders heard the remark, so she got out, humiliated and hurt, and quietly said to her husband, "You will pay for this later on tonight."

Later that night she told him how she felt, and he apologized and knew he had been very wrong. He had been in a hurry that day and hadn't used his head. He probably hadn't realized how demoralizing it was to her and how dishonored she felt.

She told him, "If you open the door for me, I'll open my door for you," referring to her sexual door. Then she said, "When you honor me publicly, I will honor you privately."

This woman was stating a very important truth. A man simply must realize that a woman needs wooing all day long, and if he mistreats her during the day or evening, she isn't going to be one bit interested in love-making that night.

Yes, the Word says we aren't to deny our spouses their rights. But the Word also says these things—hurts and disagreements—must be worked out before going to bed.

If, instead of quickly resolving this issue with her husband, this woman had withheld sex for several days or weeks just to teach him a lesson, she would have erred greatly. I know of women who do just that. They want to get even by doing the one thing that really demoralizes and punishes their husbands—withholding sexual intimacy from him. A man should never have to beg for that which really belongs to him according to God's Word.

By Using Sex To Undermine Authority

Women dominate and manipulate in many different ways. The Jezebel spirit seemed to creep into the early church when women usurped authority over men by using sex in the "spiritual doctrine." They used their bodies and sexual pleasures for the direct purpose of dominating men and credited the whole thing on a new doctrine that they claimed came from God.

In the story of Jezebel and King Ahab, sex is never mentioned, but Jezebel usurped her husband's authority as king of Israel and took things into her own hands. She also brought her religious beliefs into the land, and Ahab began worshipping her god instead of the only true God. God severely judged him for his misdeeds, and a curse was brought upon his family for generations to come.

First Kings 21:25 reveals Jezebel's wicked act of usurping her husband's authority: **But there was none like unto Ahab, which did sell himself to work wickedness in the sight of the Lord, whom Jezebel his wife stirred up.** Though Ahab was held responsible, Jezebel was the one who stirred up, and actually sought to do, the wickedness.

Though you may never have seen it as such, denying sexual intimacy or using it to get one's own way is also wickedness. Undermining your husband's authority over "his body," meaning *your* body, is wickedness. It is usurping his authority.

By Using Sex To Manipulate

Another woman who used her wiles to influence a man for evil was Delilah. The Scriptures tell us that **she pressed him daily with her words, and urged him, so that his soul was vexed unto death** (Judg. 16:16). Her words in Judges 16:15, **How canst thou say, I love thee, when thine heart is not with me?** were used to entice and manipulate him into telling her the secret behind his strength. She worked for the enemy to destroy him, and it nearly worked: It reduced him to a blind slave to the Philistines.

Although the Bible doesn't tell us specifically that she withdrew sexual pleasures from him or used them as a tool, Judges 16:13 tells us that he fell asleep on her lap. This may indicate that sexual intimacy did occur. I believe it is relatively clear that she employed sexual as well as emotional manipulation to get him to tell all.

Most women would never consider misusing sex so blatantly, but this story serves as a warning to be cautious how we use this powerful tool. Wives should always be building up their husbands, not tearing them down, demoralizing them, undermining them or manipulating them in any way.

By Using Sex To Fulfill Deceitful Intentions

While God does use the reward system to motivate us into doing right, women must be careful not to use sexual control over their husbands to get them to do things they desire.

For instance, let's say a woman really wants to buy a certain dress which her husband cannot justify buying immediately.

Promising him sexual pleasures if he buys her the dress is manipulation. She is using her sexual power to get her own way. Such manipulation is selfish and self-centered, regardless of whether she thinks buying the new dress is a necessary expenditure.

Sometimes women approach men in a way that can seem right, or even spiritual, but they have ulterior motives. It can seem as though a woman is using sexual intimacy to build up a man when, in fact, she is performing for her own benefit.

We see a good illustration of such misuse in Proverbs 7:10-23. Even though the verses are about a prostitute's seduction of a man, many wives use this same method in marriage.

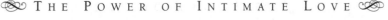

Verse 10 says that the harlot wore sexy clothing to attract him (men are turned on by sight, and there is nothing wrong with a wife doing this for her husband) but she was **subtil of heart.** The word *subtil,* or *subtle,* used here means "to keep; keep from view, hide."[5] The motives of her heart were hidden and not made known.

Verse 13 says, **She caught him, and kissed him, and with an impudent face said unto him....** To have an impudent face means "to strengthen the face or to be unveiled, as was a harlot's custom."[6] In the Jewish culture in those days, married women wore veils to signify they were under their husband's protection. Harlots "strengthened" their faces by taking off the veils. This declared boldness, and, in fact, their power over men and the accepted customs of that time.

The harlot mentioned here kisses the man to arouse him further, then makes the whole thing sound spiritual by mentioning peace offerings and vows: **I have peace offerings with me; this day have I payed my vows** (v. 14).

Next, she flatters him by saying she has been after him and has been pursuing him diligently: **Therefore came I forth to meet thee, diligently to seek thy face, and I have found thee** (v. 15). Now, since men want to be pursued at times and want to be sexually sought after, you can imagine how this affected him.

Then in verse 16, she refers to the beautiful tapestries she has placed on her couch where she reclines at meals. Then in verse 17 she verbally proceeds to her bedroom, describing how she has prepared her bed for their sexual activities with perfume, aloes and spices.[7]

In verse 18, she promises sexual pleasures that will last all night long saying, **Come, let us take our fill of love until the morning: let us solace ourselves with loves.** *Solace* means to "exult, wave joyously" and is translated as *rejoice* in other verses.[8] So she is promising a rousing good time.

She uses every means—including worship, food and the possibility of full sexual satisfaction—to incite the passions and appetites of the man she seeks to ensnare.[9] The harlot's final emotional enticement is to say that her husband has gone on a journey, so they will be uninterrupted. (vv. 19,20.)

Verse 21 says it all: **With her much fair speech she caused him to yield, with the flattering of her lips she forced him.** Clearly, this reveals ulterior motives for her flattery; her purpose is not purely to build up this man's ego.

True, this passage is speaking of how a harlot entraps a man, but some women use similar tactics on their husbands for their own selfish motives.

Men clearly need their wives to build up their egos. One definition of the word *helpmeet,* found in Genesis 2:18, is "alter ego," so it is fairly obvious that a wife, a man's other half, is to bring to her husband that which is needed.[10] But deceitful flattery for selfish purposes is not part of her responsibility.

Proverbs 31:10-12 asks: **Who can find a virtuous woman? for her price is far above rubies. The heart of her husband doth safely trust in her, so that he shall have no need of spoil. She will do him good and not evil all the days of her of her life.** First of all, that word *virtuous* means "strength, might, valor; ability of body or of mind."[11] He can safely trust in her wholeheartedly, knowing she will do only good to him. *The Amplified Version* of verse 12 uses the words *comfort* and *encourage* to describe what *doing him good* means.

Verse 11 says that the heart of her husband trusts in her and that he will have *no need of spoil.* Victorious warriors brought back *spoils* from the lands they conquered. Usually it was gold, silver and jewels. But when a man has a virtuous woman, he has a real jewel, more valuable than anyone can even put a price upon.

He can trust her when she is building him up, when she is pursuing him, when she is dressed in seductive lingerie just for him, when she is perfuming her bed and luring him into it. He doesn't need to go looking for another woman for his sexual appetites, or for any other needs, to be satisfied. For he has the greatest gem of all, and she is all his. She is withholding nothing from him and is giving of herself, body and soul, to him freely without restrictions and without deceitful intentions.

Ladies, it is so important to use this most powerful tool of sexual intimacy wisely and to be priceless, virtuous women to our husbands. Do them good and not evil all the days of their lives. Wouldn't it be wonderful for your husband to say of you, **Many daughters have done virtuously, but thou excellest them all** (v. 29). Proverbs then goes on to make this promise: **Favour is deceitful, and beauty is vain: but a woman that feareth the Lord, she shall be praised** (v. 30). Honor the Lord regarding your position as a wife, particularly in the powerful area of your sex life, and you will be honored.

THE WAYS HUSBANDS MISUSE SEX

Women are not the only people who misuse the powerful tool of sexual intimacy. Men are equally guilty of such misuse. Husbands, as you read on, you may identify with some of these examples of misuse. If so, let this be a turning point in your marriage: Let sexual intimacy become a source of strength, rather than a cause of weakness, in the fortitude of your marriage.

By Using Money To Buy Sex

Probably the most obvious example of a man's inappropriate assumptions about sex was an extremely frustrated man who called me about his wife's lack of sexual desire toward him, especially after he had "dropped $75 on a lavish dinner with her." He claimed he treated her really nicely that evening and felt she ought to "repay" him in bed. But by the time they got home, she simply rolled over and went to sleep. He was furious, to say the least.

Now, listen, if a man takes his wife out only to buy a great time in bed later that night, he may as well pay a prostitute for sexual favors. He is treating his own wife like a harlot whose favors could be bought. If your motives are impure when you take your wife out for a romantic evening, you are attempting to manipulate her.

There is always a fine line between true romance and selfish desire. Yes, women need to be romanced. And, yes, they are more apt to respond sexually after a nice evening out. But examine your motives. Did you take her out to bless her, to be with her, to share intimate moments? Or did you do it all so she would be an exciting partner in bed later on?

A woman can sense when her husband's actions are from the heart. And when they are, her desire will be to express her love in return. Whether that means sharing an intimate time in bed or cuddling with you on the couch, she will want to enjoy you and being yours.

By Using Force To Get Sex

What about the man who forces himself on his wife stating, "You're my wife, and you owe it to me." Is this use of force considered rape? Yes, I would say so. Rape is forced sex, no matter what reasons are used to justify it.

Maybe you aren't really that straightforward about it. Maybe you manipulate her by using Scriptures. This sounds like that harlot we just read about, doesn't it? She sounded very spiritual but used the Scriptures deceitfully.

By Using Sex To Get Her Agreement

What about the man who uses sex to get his way with other things around the house? What about those who wait until their wives have had a wonderful orgasm and are feeling especially loving to obtain her agreement on something he wants, like a fishing trip, a new gun or whatever, knowing full well that under other circumstances she might not agree to it. This is manipulative and is clearly a misuse of sexual intimacy for selfish purposes.

By Using Sex To Nurture Illegitimate Fantasies

What about the man who has sexual fantasies about another woman while having sex with his wife? Ed Cole calls such inappropriate behavior "vaginal masturbation."[12] Now, that is pretty blunt, but it is also pretty true. Unless your mind, your attention and your entire focus are on your wife, you aren't really making love with her but are simply using her body to fulfill the lusts of your flesh.

Jesus said that when a man lusted after a woman he was guilty of adultery in his heart. (Matt. 5:28.) What a misuse of a powerful tool that would be. A man may seem faithful to his wife, but inside, where only he and God can see, he may not be. Yes, if you are alive and male, you are bound to notice an attractive woman, but lusting after one isn't simply observing her. God's Word is clear that when we look long enough on anything, we will soon want it. So check your thoughts quickly before they get out of hand and turn into actions, either imagined or real. God doesn't seem to differentiate. Both are sin in His eyes.

Proverbs 31:3 gives this warning: **Give not thy strength unto women, nor thy ways to that which destroyeth kings.** This verse refers to a man's sexuality as his *strength.* A careful look at the definition of that word reveals that it is speaking of his "strength, might, valor; ability of body or of mind; wealth, riches; the strength or fertile vigour of a tree."[13] So, in the context of this verse, it would appear that when a man gives himself sexually to a woman he is giving her his life, strength, wealth and vigor. It is a warning against giving oneself sexually to a woman who is not one's wife, because in so doing, a man is actually giving her his life, his strength, and is opening himself up for destruction.

By Entertaining the Spirit of Lust

Some men seem to have sexual appetites that far outweigh their wives' desires. If you are one of these men, how should you deal with your desires? There are no specifics in the Bible about frequency of sex in marriage, though the Jewish law stated some. They interpreted the Bible as they saw fit, but their laws were not God's Word. Therefore, we cannot see them as such and try to strictly abide by them.

So how can you deal with the discrepancy between your own and your wife's sexual appetites? It is helpful to find out why the discrepancy exists. While a man who has an insatiable appetite for sex may be oppressed by a lustful spirit, the average man could simply have a greater desire and need for sex than his wife. This could be the result of his wife's frequent resistance to his sexual advances. Resistance produces pressure. It intensifies your desires and magnifies the need.

To a wife in this situation, I suggest that you make yourself available as often as he feels the need and see what happens. I will almost guarantee that the desires will temper and things will even out to a workable situation that both are happy with.

For the husband who is constantly frustrated because of his wife's resistance, first of all, pray. Seek God for a solution. Be certain that a spirit is not involved and that this is not simply lust. If, after prayer, you feel you simply have a very active and enlarged sexual appetite, then talk it over with your wife. Perhaps when she really understands that you have a definite need in this area and the two of you commit it to prayer, she can more easily comply.

If it is a lustful spirit you are dealing with, you need to be delivered in the name of Jesus. If you feel you need help, seek assistance from your pastor or a competent counselor. I know of one man who, because he had been molested in his teenage years, brought a lustful spirit into his marriage. He finally got free from it, and it made a great difference in his sex life. He now has a healthy sexual appetite. If his wife is resistant, however, his appetite becomes obsessive and the old feelings creep in.

In this case, she would need to be continually aware of her responsibility in helping him maintain his deliverance and in ministering to his sexual needs.

Sometimes a woman's physical stamina, work routine, metabolism or hormonal levels can complicate a couple's sexual compatibility.

Sometimes something as simple as different schedules can cause the problem. What if she is a morning person who is up at the crack of dawn but in bed by 9:30 P.M., and he is a night owl? Somewhere somebody is going to have to give a little and compromise on the time.

One man I talked to said he just liked to unwind by watching TV late at night, but unfortunately, his wife went to bed early. I suggested that he take walks with her in the evenings, especially when the weather permitted, so they could talk and he could unwind. Walking hand in hand just does something for a couple's intimacy level, especially if they can talk about the day's events or share dreams.

It might not seem very romantic, but it is that intimacy level that counts. Just being away from the home, the kids, the responsibilities and focusing on each other helps. When a man has shared his day with his wife and listened to her talk about whatever she has needed to, he is much more likely to find her interested in sharing her body with him.

Whatever your pleasure, whatever your choice, communication with good follow-up is the key to a satisfying sexual relationship in your marriage.

Proverbs 5:18-19 says, **Let thy fountain be blessed: and rejoice with the wife of thy youth. Let her be as the loving hind and pleasant roe; let her breasts satisfy thee at all times; and be thou ravished always with her love.** This verse paints a picture of a husband continually turned on to his wife. He is totally satisfied with her sexually and rejoices that he is blessed and that his fountain is blessed.

His fountain here refers to a well or an eye in the ground from which water flows. Wells are no good if they are dried up or not flowing. They are to be used but never contaminated or else the water will have a stench to it and endanger others, even causing disease and bringing death.[14]

Men, your fountain can bring blessings or curses to you and your wife. If you honor her and always attempt to bring her blessings and pleasure with that fountain, you will receive the same in return: Your rejoicing will be great and your well will continually be blessed and replenished, and the contents will bring nourishment and refreshing to both you and your wife.

But if you are always complaining about your wife, about her lack of interest in sex, about her appearance or whatever, if you are insisting on sexual activities with which she can't agree, on sex when she isn't ready or on using sex to achieve your own desires, then that well will only breed dishonor, curses, sickness in your marriage and eventual death. It will pollute rather than enrich, it will disperse disease rather than fulfillment, it will breed ill will, resentment and frustration, rather than satisfaction and health.

USE SEX TO BUILD A BEAUTIFUL MARRIAGE

Yes, sex is a powerful tool. It has a high voltage, a strong current, an electrical force that can charge your love life and cultivate intimacy in marriage to an intensely high level. Like a power saw, it can be used to cut off the enemy's tactics and build a beautiful marriage. Like a staple gun, it can bring the two of you together quicker than any glue. Like an electric sander, it can smooth off the rough edges of your marriage almost effortlessly.

God's power tool of sexual intimacy is far more powerful and more wondrous than anything man can ever dream up. On the drawing board of the heavenly throne room, God designed marital sex specifically for the two of you to share your most intimate parts with one another lovingly and fearfully in His sight, following His wise instructions and rejoicing in His wonderful pleasures.

Such powerful ecstasy cannot be measured. It is too powerful for man to accurately handle without the help of his Creator, without the plan of the One who knows all and loves us enough to entrust this powerful tool to us in our marriages. What a wonderful, powerful gift He has given us in marital sex. It is our gift to enjoy, to use and to bring glory unto Him.

Endnotes

Introduction

[1] Harrison, *Man, Husband, Father,* 110.

Chapter 1

[1] Dillow, 89-93.

[2] Wilson, 385.

[3] Barker, 1011.

[4] Halley, 277.

[5] Wilson, 28.

[6] Dillow, 31,32.

[7] Wilson, 79.

Chapter 2

[1] Webster, 320.

[2] Trumball, 223.

[3] Cole, *Sacredness of Sex for Teens,* 45.

[4] Von Kreisler, 20.

[5] Gordis, 101.

[6] Von Kreisler, 18.

[7] Ibid., 17,18.

[8] Ibid., 18,19.

[9] Ibid., 19.

[10] Ibid., 19,20.

[11] Ibid., 19.

[12] Ibid., 19.

[13] Ibid., 20.

[14] Ibid.

[15] Ibid.

Chapter 3

[1] Nelson, 38.

[2] Dillow, 32.

[3] Ibid.

Chapter 4

[1] Dillow, 104.

[2] Harrison, *Woman, Wife, Mother.*

[3] LaHaye.

[4] Wheat, 1632.

Chapter 5

[1] Dillow, 115.

[2] DeAngelis, 89.

[3] Ziglar.

[4] Dillow, 90-93.

[5] Dillow, 114.

Chapter 6

[1] Penner, 228.

[2] Vincent, 20.

[3] Ibid.

[4] Ibid., 19.

[5] Ibid., 20.

[6] Dillow, 76.

[7] Ibid.

[8] Ibid., 77.

[9] Ibid., 83.

[10] Penner, 228.

[11] Ibid., 229.

[12] Ibid., 228, 229.

Chapter 7

[1] Dillow, 132.

[2] Ibid., 132,133.

Chapter 8

[1] Gordis, 106.

[2] Strong, "Greek," entry #1850, 30.

[3] Wilson, 132.

[4] Ginzfried, 15.

[5] Wilson, 428.

[6] Ibid., 226.

[7] Dake, 645e.

[8] Strong, "Hebrew," entry #5965, 89.

[9] Dake, 645e.

[10] Mills, 20.

[11] Wilson, 469.

[12] Cole, "Straight Talk, X-Rated."

[13] Wilson, 425.

[14] Ibid.

[15] Ibid., 177.

References

Barker, Kenneth L. NIV *Study Bible.* Grand Rapids: Zondervan, 1995.

Cole, Edwin Louis. *Sacredness of Sex for Teens,* Tulsa: Harrison House, 1988.

Cole, Edwin Louis. "Straight Talk, X-Rated," (two-tape series), Dallas: Edwin Louis Cole Ministries.

Dake, Finis Jennings. *Dake's Annotated Reference Bible.* Lawrenceville, Georgia: Dake Bible Sales, 1963, 645e.

DeAngelis, Barbara. *Real Moments for Lovers.* New York: Delacorte, 1995.

Dillow, Joseph C. *Solomon on Sex.* Nashville: Thomas Nelson, 1977.

Ginzfried, Rabbi Solomon. *Code of Jewish Law, A Compilation of Jewish Laws and Customs.* Rev. ed. New York: Hebrew Publications Congress, 1987.

Gordis, Robert. *Love and Sex : A Modern Jewish Perspective.* New York: Farrer Straus Giroux, 1978.

Halley, Henry H. *Halley's Bible Handbook.* Rev. ed. Grand Rapids: Zondervan, 1979.

Harrison, Buddy. *Man, Husband, Father.* Tulsa: Harrison House, 1995.

Harrison, Pat. *Woman, Wife, Mother.* Rev. ed. Tulsa: Harrison House, 1995.

LaHaye, Tim and Beverly. *The Act of Marriage.* Rev. ed. Grand Rapids: Zondervan, 1998.

Mills, Dick. *Hearts and Flowers, Love and Romance in Marriage Partnership.* Tulsa: Harrison House.

Nelson, Tommy. *The Book of Romance.* Nashville: Thomas Nelson, 1998.

Penner, Clifford and Joyce. *The Gift of Sex.* Waco, Texas: Word, 1981.

Strong, James. *The Exhaustive Concordance of the Bible.* "Greek Dictionary of the New Testament," "Hebrew and Chaldee Dictionary of the Old Testament." McLean: MacDonald Publishing, 1978.

Trumball, H. Clay. *The Blood Covenant, A Primitive Rite and Its Bearing on Scriptures.* Kirkwood, Missouri: Impact Books, 1975.

Vincent, Marvin R. *Word Studies on the New Testament,* vol. 3 of *The Epistles of Paul.* Peabody, Massachusetts: Hendrickson, 1984.

Von Kreisler, Kristin. "The Healing Powers of Sex," *Reader's Digest,* June 1993.

Webster's New World College Dictionary, Third Edition. New York: Simon & Schuster, Inc., 1994.

Wheat, Ed and Gaye. *Intended for Pleasure.* 3d ed. Old Tappan, NJ: Fleming H. Revell, 1997.

Wilson, William. *Old Testament Word Studies.* Grand Rapids, Michigan: Kregel, 1980.

Ziglar, Zig. Sermon. International Family Church Conference. June 1983.

Additional copies of this book

are available from your local bookstore.

HARRISON HOUSE

Tulsa, Oklahoma 74153

The Harrison House Vision

Proclaiming the truth and the power

Of the Gospel of Jesus Christ

With Excellence;

Challenging Christians to

Live victoriously,

Grow spiritually,

Know God intimately.